Cambridge English

OFFICIAL
PREPARATION MATERIAL

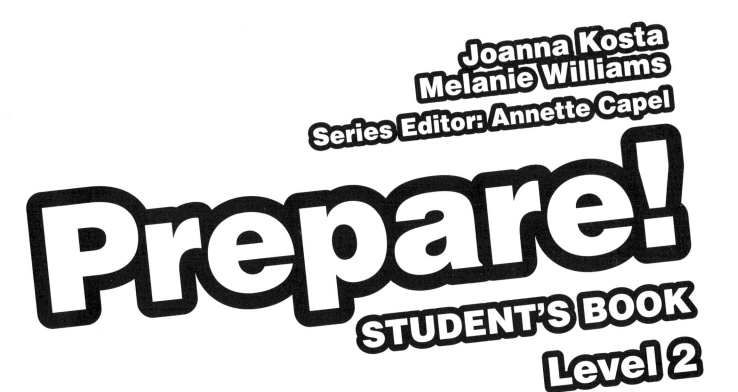

Joanna Kosta
Melanie Williams
Series Editor: Annette Capel

Prepare!
STUDENT'S BOOK
Level 2

Cambridge University Press
www.cambridge.org/elt

Cambridge English Language Assessment
www.cambridgeenglish.org

Information on this title: www.cambridge.org/9780521180481
© Cambridge University Press and UCLES 2015

First published 2015

Printed in Italy by Rotolito Lombarda S.p.A.

A catalogue record for this publication is available from the British Library

ISBN 978-0-521-18048-1 Student's Book
ISBN 978-1-107-49720-7 Student's Book and Online Workbook
ISBN 978-0-521-18049-8 Workbook with Audio
ISBN 978-0-521-18050-4 Teacher's Book with DVD and Teacher's Resources Online
ISBN 978-0-521-18052-8 Class Audio CDs
ISBN 978-1-107-49718-4 Presentation Plus DVD-ROM

Contents

READING	LISTENING	SPEAKING	WRITING	VIDEO
Restaurant menus *Street food around the world*	Booking a restaurant for a party Ordering street food at a festival	Compare restaurants and choose a restaurant for your party Ask about and order food at a street-food festival ⓔⓟ **Get talking!** *Sure, no problem, Oh no, that's too …*	An advertisement for a party	Street foods
Computers and the modern world Did you know …? – facts about computers	Andy talks about his new computer	Compare mobile phones Make true statements Computer survey	An email	Technology
Yes, you can run 5 km in six weeks!	Patients describe their problems and the doctor gives advice Advice about getting fit for a race	Talk about a health problem you had Give advice about health ⓔⓟ **Get talking!** *Oh dear, Never mind.*	Give advice on a chat page	Health problems
Visit Edinburgh	Following directions A visit to Edinburgh	Give directions Talk about visiting cities	Write and understand directions A city guide	
Are they real?	Weather in different parts of the world The Loch Ness Monster	Talk about the weather Say what you were doing at different times in the past ⓔⓟ **Get talking!** *Right, So …*	An article about a strange animal that people have seen	
A lucky day	Gary talks about his animal helper	Tell a story from pictures Say what animals your family has	An email to a friend	Animals
Talent shows	Clyde invites Mina to a concert Sandra and Ben talk about *The X Factor*	Talk about future plans Talk about talent shows ⓔⓟ **Get talking!** *Would you like to …? How about …?*	Write about a TV show you like and describe one of the actors or winners	
Two reviews	Planning a school magazine A review for a school magazine	Plan a class magazine Tell the story of a film, play or book ⓔⓟ **Get talking!** *Cool! Sounds good.*	A review	Books we like
A different way to learn	Information about the school trip A boarding school	Talk about activities on school trips Ask and answer about what you have to / don't have to do this weekend Give opinions	An article about your perfect school	School life
My family tree A really big family	Three young people talk about who they live with	Give information about a member of your family Talk about your family, big families and Mother's Day	A description of your family	

Activities page 129   **Vocabulary list** page 132   **Grammar reference** page 142   **List of irregular verbs** page 163

Welcome to *Prepare!*

Learn about the features in your new Student's Book

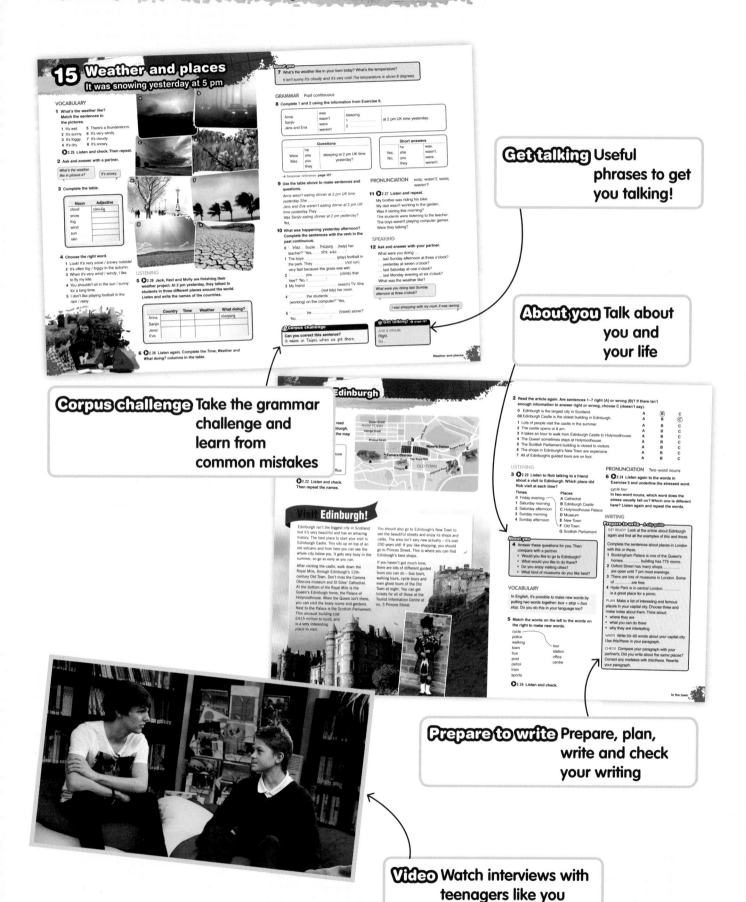

Get talking Useful phrases to get you talking!

About you Talk about you and your life

Corpus challenge Take the grammar challenge and learn from common mistakes

Prepare to write Prepare, plan, write and check your writing

Video Watch interviews with teenagers like you

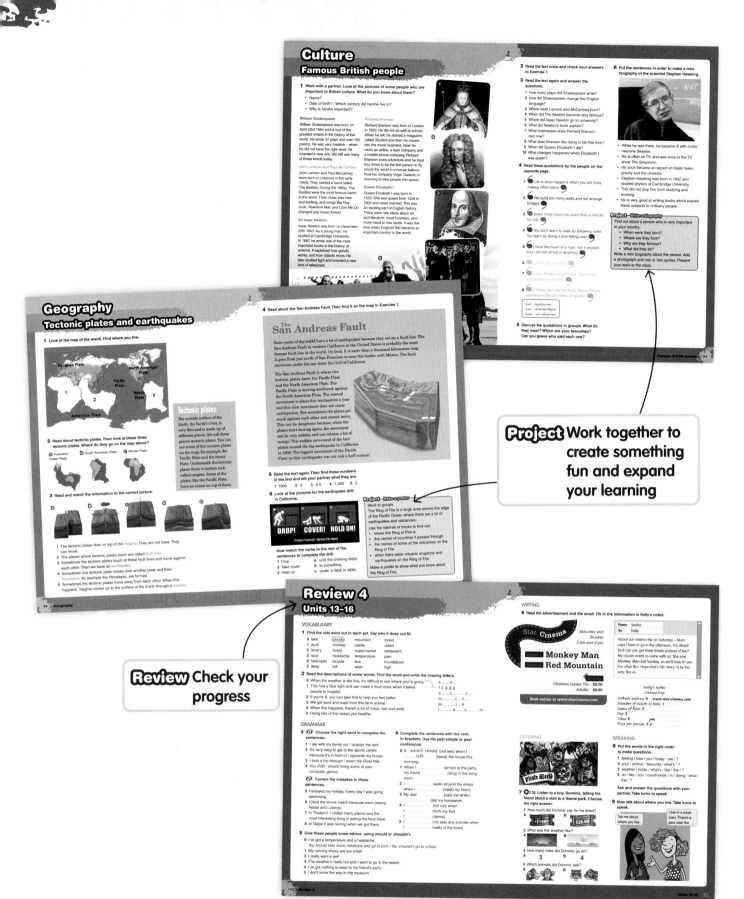

Culture
Famous British people

1 Work with a partner. Look at the pictures of some people who are important to British culture. What do you know about them?
- Name?
- Date of birth? / Which century did he/she live in?
- Why is he/she important?

William Shakespeare
William Shakespeare was born on April 23rd 1564 and is one of the greatest writers in the history of the world. He wrote 37 plays and over 150 poems. He was very creative – when he did not have the right word, he invented a new one. We still use many of these words today.

John Lennon and Paul McCartney
John Lennon and Paul McCartney were born in Liverpool in the early 1940s. They started a band called The Beatles. During the 1960s, The Beatles were the most famous band in the world. Their music was new and exciting, and songs like Hey Jude, Nowhere Man and Love Me Do changed pop music forever.

Sir Isaac Newton
Isaac Newton was born on December 25th 1643. As a young man, he studied at Cambridge University. In 1687, he wrote one of the most important books in the history of science. It explained how gravity works, and how objects move. He also studied light and invented a new kind of telescope.

Richard Branson
Richard Branson was born in London in 1950. He did not do well at school. When he left, he started a magazine called Student and then he moved into the music business. Now he owns an airline, a train company and a mobile phone company. Richard Branson loves adventure and he tried four times to be the first person to fly round the world in a hot-air balloon. Now his company Virgin Galactic is planning to take people into space.

Queen Elizabeth I
Queen Elizabeth I was born in 1533. She was queen from 1558 to 1603 and never married. This was an exciting part of English history. There were new ideas about art and literature, more business, and more travel to new lands. It was the time when England first became an important country in the world.

2 Read the text once and check your answers to Exercise 1.

3 Read the text again and answer the questions.
1 How many plays did Shakespeare write?
2 How did Shakespeare change the English language?
3 Where were Lennon and McCartney born?
4 When did The Beatles become very famous?
5 Where did Isaac Newton go to university?
6 What did Newton's book explain?
7 What businesses does Richard Branson own now?
8 What does Branson like doing in his free time?
9 When did Queen Elizabeth I die?
10 What changes happened when Elizabeth I was queen?

4 Read these quotations by the people on the opposite page.
1 Life is what happens when you are busy making other plans.
2 We build too many walls and not enough bridges.
3 Better three hours too soon than a minute too late.
4 You don't learn to walk by following rules. You learn by doing it and falling over.
5 I have the heart of a man, not a woman. And I am not afraid of anything.
6 *[illegible]*
7 A fool thinks himself wise, but a wise man knows he is a fool.
8 If I have seen further than others, it is by standing on the shoulders of giants.

fool – stupid person
wise – clever/intelligent
giant – very tall person

5 Discuss the quotations in groups. What do they mean? Which are your favourites? Can you guess who said each one?

6 Put the sentences in order to make a mini biography of the scientist Stephen Hawking.
- While he was there, he became ill with motor neurone disease.
- He is often on TV, and was once in the TV show The Simpsons.
- He soon became an expert on black holes, gravity and the universe.
- Stephen Hawking was born in 1942 and studied physics at Cambridge University.
- This did not stop him from studying and working.
- He is very good at writing books which explain these subjects to ordinary people.

Project Write a biography
Find out about a person who is very important in your country.
- When were they born?
- Where are they from?
- Why are they famous?
- What did they do?
Write a mini biography about the person. Add a photograph and one or two quotes. Present your work to the class.

Geography
Tectonic plates and earthquakes

1 Look at the map of the world. Find where you live.

Eurasian Plate
North American Plate
Pacific Plate
Nazca Plate
Antarctica Plate

Tectonic plates
The outside surface of the Earth, the Earth's crust, is very thin and is made up of different pieces. We call these pieces tectonic plates. You can see some of the tectonic plates on the map, for example the Pacific Plate and the Nazca Plate. Underneath the tectonic plates there is molten rock called magma. Some of the plates, like the Pacific Plate, have an ocean on top of them.

2 Read about tectonic plates. Then look at these three tectonic plates. Where do they go on the map above?
a Australian-Indian Plate
b South American Plate
c African Plate

3 Read and match the information to the correct picture.
a b c d e
1 The tectonic plates float on top of magma. They are not fixed. They can move.
2 The places where tectonic plates touch are called fault lines.
3 Sometimes the tectonic plates touch at these fault lines and move against each other. Then we have an earthquake.
4 Sometimes one tectonic plate moves over another plate and then mountains, for example the Himalayas, are formed.
5 Sometimes the tectonic plates move away from each other. When this happens, magma comes up to the surface of the Earth through a volcano.

4 Read about the San Andreas Fault. Then find it on the map in Exercise 1.

The San Andreas Fault

Some parts of the world have a lot of earthquakes because they are on a fault line. The San Andreas Fault in western California in the United States is probably the most famous fault line in the world. On land, it is more than a thousand kilometres long. It goes from just north of San Francisco to near the border with Mexico. The fault continues under the sea down the Gulf of California.

The San Andreas Fault is where two tectonic plates meet: the Pacific Plate and the North American Plate. The Pacific Plate is moving northwest against the North American Plate. The normal movement is about five centimetres a year and this slow movement does not cause earthquakes. But sometimes the plates get stuck against each other and cannot move. This can be dangerous because, when the plates start moving again, the movement can be very sudden and can release a lot of energy. This sudden movement of the two plates caused the big earthquake in California in 1906. The biggest movement of the Pacific Plate in that earthquake was six and a half metres!

5 Read the text again. Then find these numbers in the text and tell your partner what they are.
1 1906   2 5   3 6.5   4 1,000   5 2

6 Look at the pictures for the earthquake drill in California.

DROP!   COVER!   HOLD ON!
Protect Yourself. Spread The Word

Now match the verbs to the rest of the sentences to complete the drill.
1 Drop   a until the shaking stops.
2 Take cover   b under a desk or table.
3 Hold on   c on your hands and knees.

Project Make a poster
Work in groups.
The Ring of Fire is a large area around the edge of the Pacific Ocean where there are a lot of earthquakes and volcanoes.
Use the internet or books to find out:
- where the Ring of Fire is
- the names of countries it passes through
- the names of some of the volcanoes on the Ring of Fire
- when there were volcanic eruptions and earthquakes on the Ring of Fire.
Make a poster to show what you know about the Ring of Fire.

Project Work together to create something fun and expand your learning

Review 4
Units 13–16

Review Check your progress

VOCABULARY
1 Find the odd word out in each set. Say why it does not fit.
0 lake   (cloudy)   mountain   forest
1 duck   monkey   castle   rabbit
2 library   forest   supermarket   restaurant
3 race   headache   temperature   pain
4 helicopter   bicycle   bus   roundabout
5 deep   left   wide   high

2 Read the descriptions of some words. Find the word and write the missing letters.
0 When the weather is like this, it's difficult to see where you're going.   s _ _ e
1 This has a blue light and can make a loud noise when it takes people to hospital.   f _ _ g _ _ g _
2 If you're ill, you can take this to help you feel better.   m _ _ u _ _ _ e
3 We get wool and meat from this farm animal.   a _ _ _ _ _
4 When this happens, there's a lot of noise, rain and wind.   ex _ _ _ _ i _ e
5 Doing lots of this keeps you healthy.   t _ _ _ _ d _ _ s _ _ _ m

GRAMMAR
3 Choose the right word to complete the sentences.
1 I ate with my family out / outside the tent.
2 It's very easy to get to the sports centre because it's in front of / opposite my house.
3 I took a trip through / down the River Nile.
4 You shall / should bring some of your computer games.

Correct the mistakes in these sentences.
5 I enjoyed my holiday. Every day I was going swimming.
6 I liked the tennis match because were playing Nadal and Loranzo.
7 In Thailand, I visited many places and the most interesting thing is eating the food there.
8 In Taipei it was raining when we got there.

4 Complete the sentences with the verb in brackets. Use the past simple or past continuous.
0 It _wasn't raining_ (not rain) when I _left_ (leave) the house this morning.
1 When I _____ (arrive) at the party, my friend _____ (sing) in the living room.
2 I _____ (walk) around the shops when I _____ (meet) my friend.
3 My dad _____ (call) me while I _____ (do) my homework.
4 I _____ (not run) when I _____ (hurt) my foot.
5 I _____ (dance).
6 I _____ (not see) any animals when I _____ (walk) in the forest.

5 Give these people some advice, using should or shouldn't.
0 I've got a temperature and a headache.
You should take some medicine and go to bed. / You shouldn't go to school.
1 My running shoes are too small.
2 I really want a pet!
3 The weather's really hot and I want to go to the beach.
4 I've got nothing to wear to my friend's party.
5 I don't know the way to the museum.

WRITING
6 Read the advertisement and the email. Fill in the information in Kelly's notes.

Star Cinema
Saturday and Sunday
2 pm and 8 pm
Monkey Man
Red Mountain
Children (under 15) - £6.00
Adults - £8.50
Book online at www.starcinema.com

From: Sasha
To: Kelly
About our cinema trip on Saturday – Mum says I have to go in the afternoon, I'm afraid! And can you get three tickets instead of two? My cousin wants to come with us. She saw Monkey Man last Sunday, so we'll have to see the other film. Hope that's OK! She's 13 by the way, like us.

Kelly's notes
Cinema trip
Website address: 0   www.starcinema.com
Number of tickets to book: 1
Name of film: 2
Day: 3
Time: 4   pm
Price per person: 5 £

LISTENING
7 2.35 Listen to a boy, Dominic, telling his friend about a visit to a theme park. Choose the right answer.
1 How much did Dominic pay for his ticket?
A Free   B £25.00
2 What was the weather like?
A   B   C
3 How many rides did Dominic go on?
A 3   B 4
4 Which animals did Dominic see?
A   B   C

SPEAKING
8 Put the words in the right order to make questions.
1 feeling / how / you / today / are / ?
2 your / animal / favourite / what's / ?
3 weather / today / what's / like / the / ?
4 do / like / you / countryside / in / doing / what / the / ?
Ask and answer the questions with your partner. Take turns to speak.

9 Now talk about where you live. Take turns to speak.
Tell me about where you live.
I live in a small town. There's a park near the ...

Look through your book and do the quiz with your partner.
1 What is the topic of Unit 3?
2 How many colours can you see on page 58?
3 In which unit can you find the capital of Scotland?
4 How many animals are there on page 94?
5 Can you find a famous runner? What page is he on?

Get started!
In the classroom

THINGS IN THE CLASSROOM

1 Match each word in the box to the correct letter.

> bag   board   chair   coat   computer   door   exercise book   map
> pencil case   pens   poster   rubber   ruler   teacher   textbook   window

2 What colour is each thing? Write five sentences. Compare your sentences with your partner.

The coat is blue.   The door is white.
The pens are blue and black.

> **Verb *be***
> I **am**   he/she/it **is**   you/we/they **are**

THERE IS / THERE ARE

3 Look at the picture and read the sentences. Write *yes* or *no*.

0 There's a rubber on the table.   *yes*
1 There are five students in the classroom.
2 There's a red pencil case on the table.
3 There's a blue bag on a chair

4 There's a computer near the window.
5 There's a poster on the wall.
6 There's a bag on the floor.

4 ▶1.02 Listen to the questions. Put a tick (✔) under the correct answer for each question.

	Yes, there is.	Yes, there are.	No, there isn't.	No there aren't.
1				
2				
3				
4				
5				

5 Work with a partner.
Student A: Look around the classroom for 60 seconds, and then close your eyes.
Student B: Ask questions about the classroom.

B: Is there a green bag under my desk?   *A: Yes, there is. / No, there isn't.*

HAVE GOT

6 Read what Simon says. Tick (✔) the things he's got in his bag.

> My bag's really heavy today! I've got four textbooks, three exercise books and my pencil case. I've also got a big bottle of water because I've got football club after school. I've got a sandwich and some money too. I haven't got my phone – that's at home in my bedroom.

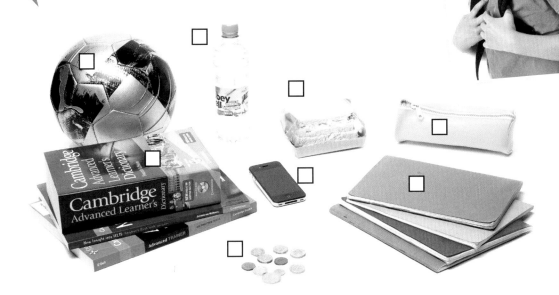

7 Ask and answer with your partner.

A: What have you got in your bag today?
B: I've got ....
A: Have you got a/an/any .... in your bag today?
B: Yes, I have. / No, I haven't.

Write five sentences about your partner.

THE ALPHABET

A a B b C c D d E e F f

G g H h I i J j K k L l

M m N n O o P p Q q R r

S s T t U u V v W w X x

Y y Z z

8 ▶ 1.03 Listen and repeat.

9 Work with a partner. Complete the table with letters that have the same sound. Two columns have no other letters!

A	B	F	I	O	U	R
H	C					

SPEAKING

10 Complete sentences 1–5 with words from the box. Then match each question to an answer a–e.

> page   borrow   say   repeat   spell

1 I'm sorry, can you .... that, please?
2 How do you .... 'bonjour' in English?
3 What .... are we on?
4 How do you .... 'because'?
5 Can I .... your ruler?

a B-E-C-A-U-S-E.
b Sure, here you are.
c I said, please do Exercise 3.
d 19, I think.
e Hello.

Talk about you

NUMBERS

1 ▶1.04 Listen and repeat.

1 one	2 two	3 three	4 four	5 five
6 six	7 seven	8 eight	9 nine	10 ten
11 eleven	12 twelve	13 thirteen	14 fourteen	15 fifteen
16 sixteen	17 seventeen	18 eighteen	19 nineteen	20 twenty

2 ▶1.05 Listen and circle the right number.

a	25	75	39
b	13	30	70
c	41	61	91
d	14	16	40
e	17	19	90
f	15	50	80

DATES

3 Say the months in the correct order.

November   September   March   January

May   December   August   July

February   October   April   June

January …

▶1.06 Listen and check.

4 ▶1.07 Listen and write the dates.

> When we **write** dates, we **omit** *the* and *of*:
> *My birthday is on 9th June.*
> When we **say** dates, we **say** *the* and *of*:
> *My birthday is on **the** ninth **of** June.*

a .... 1st March ....
b ....
c ....
d ....
e ....
f ....
g ....
h ....

MON	TUES	WEDS	THURS	FRI	SAT	SUN
1st	2nd	3rd	4th	5th	6th	7th
8th	9th	10th	11th	12th	13th	14th
15th	16th	17th	18th	19th	20th	21st
22nd	23rd	24th	25th	26th	27th	28th
29th	30th	31st				

Check with your partner. Say the dates.

5 Work in groups of four. Make questions. Ask and answer. Take turns.

- When / your birthday?
- What / today's date?
- When / your mum's/dad's birthday?

Write the other students' dates in your exercise book.

CAN

6 Match the words to the pictures.

> draw a car   make a cake   play tennis   ride a bike   run 5km
> speak three languages   stand on your head   swim under water

7 Work with a partner. Ask and answer using *can*.

Now ask around the class.
How many people can …

- swim under water?
- speak three languages?
- ride a bike?
- play tennis?
- draw a car?

> Can you swim under water?
>
> No, I can't.
>
> Can you play tennis?
>
> Yes, I can.

PRESENT SIMPLE

8 Read about the students and answer the questions. Use complete sentences.

> Hi, my name's Jack. I've got a brother and a sister. I like music and I love travelling. I want to go to China.

> Hello, I'm Ravi. I haven't got any brothers or sisters. I like all sports and I play football every day.

> Hello, my name's Molly. I like swimming and I often go shopping with my sister on Saturday. I love sweets but I don't like ice cream.

1 Does Jack like music?
2 How many brothers has Ravi got?
3 What sport does Molly like?
4 Where does Jack want to go?
5 What does Ravi do every day?
6 When does Molly go shopping?

9 Work with a partner. Ask and answer.

A: *Do you do sports every day?*
B: *Yes, I do. I play tennis after school every day.*

1 do sports / every day?
2 what kind of music / like?
3 like travelling?
4 play football at school?
5 like swimming?
6 What / favourite / food?

Now tell the class.

Manuela doesn't do sports every day. She likes …

SPEAKING

10 Write questions to find out about your partner's …

- age
- address
- phone number
- brothers and sisters
- favourite pop star
- favourite school subject

Ask and answer with your partner. Then write about them.

1 Sports and games
I'm never bored

VOCABULARY

1 Which of these sports do you know? Match them to the pictures.

> rugby   badminton   sailing   baseball   snowboarding
> volleyball   cycling   skating   running   hockey

play

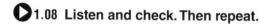

go

▶ **1.08** Listen and check. Then repeat.

2 Ask and answer with your partner.

1 Which of the sports do you do in teams?
You play volleyball and … in teams.
2 Which of the sports do you do alone?
3 Which of the sports can you do both in teams and alone?

4 Which of these sports do *you* do?
5 Do you prefer team sports or sports you do alone? Why?

READING

3 Read about Jess and James. Who wants to win at the Olympics? Who does their sport in other countries?

Two young sports stars

Jess Barnes received the Young Sailor of the Year award and she was only 13!

'It's amazing,' says Jess. 'I love sailing. It's my life. I always go sailing at weekends. I'm never bored. I sometimes go sailing in a team but I go sailing alone, too. In the holidays, I usually go to different sailing competitions. Some of these are in other countries. It's difficult to get a place in the competition teams. I need to work hard but I know I can do it! I want to sail and to win.'

Jess

'I didn't like playing rugby and football. They're boring! I wanted to try a different sport. Cycling is different and no one else at my school does it,' says **James Miller**.

'I really love the sport and it keeps me fit. I often go cycling with my friends. It's good practice for my team competitions. I'm sometimes tired but then I think about the Olympics. I want to go there and win! Remember – you don't find many world champions on the sofa!'

James

4 **Read about Jess and James again and answer the questions.**

1 What does Jess do on Saturdays and Sundays?
2 Does Jess go sailing alone or in a team?
3 Why does Jess need to work hard?
4 What does James think of rugby and football?
5 How many people at James's school go cycling?
6 What helps James when he is tired?

PRONUNCIATION /eɪ/ and /aɪ/

5 **Put the words into the right column of the table.**

| ~~baseball~~ | bike | day | fly |
| life | riding | skating | wait |

/eɪ/ **sailing**	/aɪ/ **cycling**
baseball	

▶ 1.09 **Listen and check. Then repeat.**

GRAMMAR Adverbs of frequency

We use the present simple to talk about things we do often or every day.
*I **go** sailing alone, too.*

6 **Look at these examples from the texts. The adverbs of frequency are in red.**

I always go sailing at weekends.
I'm never bored.
I usually go to different sailing competitions.
I often go cycling with my friends.
I'm sometimes tired.

Which sentences have a present simple verb?
Which sentences have the verb *be*?
Choose the right words to complete the rules.

In sentences with the **verb *be***, we put the adverb of frequency *before* / *after* the **verb**.
In sentences with the **present simple**, we put the adverb of frequency *before* / *after* the **verb**.

→ Grammar reference **page 143**

7 **Look at these other examples.**

People don't always play sport in teams.
Sarah doesn't usually go sailing in the evenings.
Do you sometimes go sailing with friends?
Is cycling often dangerous?
Football isn't always boring!

Choose the right words to complete the rules.

In negatives and questions with the **present simple,** we put the adverb of frequency *before* / *after* the **main verb**.
In negatives and questions with the **verb *be*,** we put the adverb of frequency *before* / *after* the **adjective**.

8 **Read the examples from Exercise 6 and write the words in red next to the right picture.**

1 .... 4 ....
2 .... 5 ....
3 ....

9 **How often do you do the sports in Exercise 1? Ask and answer with your partner.**

A: *I never play rugby but I often play football. It's great fun. How about you?*
B: *I sometimes play rugby and I often go running. It's never boring.*

⟳ Corpus challenge

Can you correct this sentence? Choose the right answer.
I drink juice always.
A I drink always juice.
B I always drink juice.
C I always juice drink.

SPEAKING

10 **You are a young sports star. Answer these questions. Make notes.**

1 What sport do you do?
2 Do you do this sport alone or in a team?
3 When do you do this sport?
4 How often do you travel to competitions?
5 Is this a difficult sport to learn and do? Why?
6 What competitions do you want to win?

11 **Work with a partner. Student A: Ask Student B questions 2–6. Don't ask question 1!**
Student B: Answer the questions.
Student A: Guess the sport. Then change roles.

How do you play it?

READING

1 Look at the pictures of the five sports and games. What can you see?

2 Read the texts and match each one to a picture.

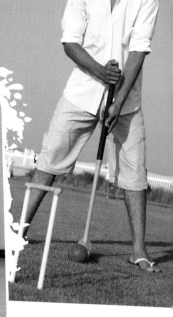

1 Octopush

This sport is also called underwater hockey. There are two teams. Each team has got six players. Players swim underwater. They try to hit the heavy ball into the other team's goal. The winning team is the team with the most goals at the end of the match.

2 Futsal

This sport is like football. There are two teams. Each team has got five players. Players kick the ball and try to get a goal. The ball is smaller than a football. Players usually play the game inside.

3 Croquet

People play this game on grass. There are four balls of different colours. Players don't play in teams. They play singles or doubles. Players hit the balls through hoops on the grass. The winner is the first player to hit all the balls through all the hoops.

3 Read the three texts again. Are the sentences right (✔) or wrong (✗)?

1 Octopush is like volleyball.
2 People play octopush in teams.
3 Octopush players are good at swimming.
4 There are five players in a game of futsal.
5 Futsal players never use a bat.

6 A futsal ball is the same as a football.
7 People play croquet outside.
8 In croquet, there are two teams.
9 Croquet players kick the balls with their feet.

4 ▶1.10 **Two people are talking about the other two sports and games. Listen and match them to the two pictures.**

5 ▶1.10 **Listen again. Tick (✔) the correct sentences about the games.**

	Pelota	Cheese rolling
1 It's a game.		
2 It's an old sport.	✔	
3 People run down a hill.		
4 People hit the ball with their hands.		
5 People play in teams.		
6 Only one person is the winner.		
7 The winner can take the food home.		
8 People play inside.		

VOCABULARY

6 **Put the sports in the right box in the diagram.**

badminton ~~baseball~~ basketball ~~cycling~~ football hockey rugby running sailing skating snowboarding swimming table tennis tennis ~~volleyball~~

baseball

volleyball baseball

use a bat, a racket or a stick   use a ball

do it in teams   do it alone or in teams

volleyball baseball

cycling

7 **Read the sentences about Rob's favourite sport. Choose the best word (A, B or C) for each space.**

0 Rob's favourite sport ..A.. hockey.
   A is   **B** likes   **C** does

1 He's got a new hockey ....
   A bat   **B** stick   **C** racket

2 He .... hockey every day after school.
   A plays   **B** goes   **C** works

3 Rob is in the school hockey .... , too.
   A group   **B** player   **C** team

4 There is a .... every Saturday.
   A match   **B** sport   **C** group

5 Every week, Rob gets lots of ....
   A competitions **B** champions **C** goals

About you

8 What unusual sports or games do you know? How do you play them? Does your country have a special game?

WRITING

9 **Work in groups of four. Choose a sport or a game. What do you do? How do you play it? Talk about your ideas. Make notes.**

10 **Work alone. Write five sentences about the sport or game. Use the texts from Exercise 2 to help you. Find a picture of your game on the internet. Include it under your text.**

2 Tastes wonderful!
Today I'm making pancakes

a ☐ b ☐ c ☐ d ☐ e ☐ f ☐ g ☐

VOCABULARY

1 Look at picture a. Match the things 1–7 to the words in the box.

> a bowl   chocolate sauce   cream
> fresh fruit   a lemon   oil   a pan

▶ 1.11 Listen and check. Then repeat.

LISTENING

2 ▶ 1.12 Listen to a boy, James, talking about how to make pancakes. Number pictures b–g in the correct order.

3 Complete the recipe with the words and numbers in the box.

> 300 ml   Mix   Two   Serve
> Cook   100 g   Put   Add

▶ 1.12 Listen again and check your answers.

Pancakes

You need:
.... eggs
.... milk
.... flour

How to make them
1 .... the eggs and milk together.
2 .... the eggs and milk to the flour.
3 .... some oil in a pan.
4 .... the pancake on both sides.
5 .... it with lemon and sugar, or chocolate sauce, fresh fruit and cream.

GRAMMAR Present continuous and present simple

4 Look at these examples from the listening. Write *simple* or *continuous*.

> **Present** ....
>
> I'm cooking the first pancake <u>now</u>.
> I'm mixing the milk and eggs <u>at the moment</u>.
> I'm serving this one with chocolate sauce and fresh fruit <u>today</u>.

> **Present** ....
>
> I <u>never</u> use water.
> I <u>always</u> make my pancakes very thin.
> I <u>always</u> mix it really well.
> I <u>usually</u> serve pancakes with lemon and sugar.

→ Grammar reference **page 144**

5 Look at the <u>underlined</u> words in the table and complete the rules.

> We often use the present simple with words like .... , ... and ....
> We often use the present continuous with words like .... , ... and ....

6 Put the verb in the correct tense.

0 I ...'m shopping... (shop) at the moment. I can't talk.

1 My mum always .... (cook) nice food.

2 The teachers usually .... (give) us a lot of homework on Monday.

3 I .... (stay) at home today.
   I .... (not go) to school.

4 It's three o'clock now and I .... (watch) TV with my sister.

5 My dad often .... (get up) late on Sunday.

6 At the moment, we .... (have) lunch. Ring me again later.

Corpus challenge

Can you correct this sentence?
Choose the right answer.

How are you? I ~~write~~ to you to give you some news.

A writes   **B** am writing   **C** writing

READING

7 Look at the pictures. What are the people doing?

8 Read the text. Match each paragraph to a picture.

Pancake Day

Shrove Tuesday, called Pancake Day in Britain, happens 41 days before Easter Sunday. For the next 40 days, some people don't eat sweets, chocolates or crisps. But on Pancake Day, they can eat as many pancakes as they want.

In many villages, people have pancake races. In Olney, the married women run a race. They carry a pancake in a pan and run for 400 metres.

In France, this day is a festival called Mardi Gras. This means Fat Tuesday. People wear amazing clothes and go out in the streets to have fun. It is also called Mardi Gras in New Orleans and this festival is famous all over the world.

About you

9 Do you have Shrove Tuesday in your country?

Yes
What do you call it?

No
Think of a festival in your country.

What do you eat?   What do you wear?
What do you do?

Lunch is always at midday

READING AND VOCABULARY

1 Read about what three teenagers from different countries eat. Match the pictures to the words in the box.

> cabbage   cereal   chilli   cucumber
> curry and rice   fruit tea   honey
> hot chocolate   jam   mango   salad
> toast   yogurt

▶ 1.13 **Listen and check. Then repeat.**

2 Find these words in the texts.

0 This is the first meal of the day. breakfast
1 This is sweet and you have it at the end of the meal.
2 You have this when you don't need a big meal.
3 You have this meal in the middle of the day.
4 You have this at the beginning of a meal.
5 This is the last meal of the day.

TELL US WHAT YOU EAT

Luigi – Italy

In the morning, I have cake, or fruit and yogurt. I usually have a glass of milk but my sister has hot chocolate. I have my main meal of the day at lunchtime – usually between 12 and 1 o'clock. The first course is pasta with a nice sauce, and then we have meat or fish with vegetables. Often for dessert we have ice cream but not every day. My favourite is tutti frutti. That means 'all the fruits' in Italian. It tastes wonderful!

Jan – Slovakia

Sometimes I have cereal for breakfast but it's usually bread and butter with cold meat or cheese. I have that with tomatoes and cucumber. To drink I have fruit tea with sugar. Lunch is the main meal of the day and it's always at midday. For the first course, we have soup. I like cabbage soup best but chicken soup is good too. For the main course, we have meat with potatoes or rice, and maybe some salad. We don't have a dessert at lunchtime. In the evening, we never have a big meal. We just have a snack.

Arjan – Britain

I always have cereal with milk and sugar for breakfast but my sister has toast and jam or honey. We both drink tea. Lunch is at about 12.30. I usually have a sandwich, some crisps and some juice or water. We have supper in the evening, at about 6 o'clock. My favourite is curry and rice. Mum makes a salad of chilli and mango to go with it. It's really nice.

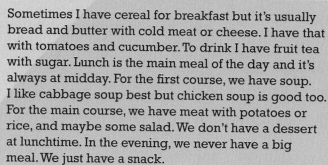

3 Read the texts again. For questions 1–6, choose A, B or C: **A** Luigi   **B** Jan   **C** Arjan.

0 Who has his main meal in the evening? C
1 Who doesn't have two courses at lunchtime?
2 Who always has lunch at the same time every day?
3 Who doesn't have a hot lunch?
4 Who has a different drink from his sister at breakfast?
5 Who doesn't usually eat sweet food for breakfast?
6 Who sometimes has three courses for his lunch?

PRONUNCIATION The sound /ə/

4 ▶ 1.14 **Listen and repeat. These words have the sound /ə/ in them.**

> breakfast   famous   lemonade

5 ▶ 1.15 **Listen and repeat. Circle the /ə/ sound in each word. One word has two /ə/ sounds. Which word is it?**

> pasta   chocolate   banana   salad   festival
> tomato   yogurt   cucumber

LISTENING AND SPEAKING

6 ▶ 1.16 **Listen to the radio show. What is each person having for lunch? Write M, R or J next to each picture 1–9.**

Molly   Ravi   Jack

7 Ask and answer these questions with your partner.

- Are Molly, Ravi and Jack's lunches healthy?
- Do you have lunch at school or at home?
- What do you have for lunch? Is it a healthy lunch?

EP Get talking! → page 124

> Tell me about …
> It's … . What about you?
> Well, I …

WRITING

Prepare to write — A message on the internet

GET READY Read the three texts again and find all the examples of *and*, *but* and *or*.

Choose the right word to complete the sentence.

0 We don't get chocolate ......or...... crisps at school.   *or / but*
1 I don't eat breakfast .... I have a big lunch.   *but / or*
2 I eat lots of fruit .... drink lots of water.   *and / or*
3 I have cake in the morning .... I don't have it in the evening.   *but / and*
4 I don't like carrots .... tomatoes.   *or / but*

PLAN Think about what you eat every day. Make some notes.

	time?	food?	drink?
breakfast			
lunch			
supper			

WRITE Write a paragraph about what you eat every day. Use *and*, *but* and *or*.

IMPROVE Read your paragraph and your partner's. Check for mistakes and try to make your paragraph better.

Culture
Festivals

1 Look at the pictures and the names of the festivals. What do you know about these festivals?

The Moon Festival

This is an important festival in China and Vietnam. It happens every year in September or early October, when the moon is full. In Vietnam, there are parades in the streets. Children wear special masks and carry beautiful lights called lanterns. In some parts of China, people dress up as dragons. Family and friends get together for a meal and spend time looking at the moon. Everyone eats moon cakes. These are sweet, and often have an egg in the middle of them.

Diwali

Diwali is the Hindu festival of lights. It lasts for five days and celebrates the New Year. It happens in October or November. People light hundreds of small lamps and put them in their homes and gardens. This is to bring good luck and to welcome the goddess Lakshmi into their home. Food is an important part of the festival and people make special sweets to share. They wear bright clothes and jewellery. They decorate their homes with flowers, and draw patterns with rice flour at the entrance of the home. People also give gifts and let off fireworks during Diwali.

2 Read the texts and look at the pictures. Match the words to the descriptions.

1 a mask
2 a dragon
3 a lamp
4 decorate
5 bring good luck
6 a wish
7 a firework
8 a gift
9 a parade
10 dress up

a You do this to make something look pretty.
b This is something you want to happen.
c This is what you do when you put on special clothes.
d This is a kind of monster.
e This makes a loud noise and bright colours in the sky.
f You wear this over your face.
g This is a kind of light. You can carry it in your hand.
h This is a line of people moving down the street.
i If something does this, it makes nice things happen.
j You give this to someone – it's the same as a present.

3 Read the texts again and complete the table.

	The Moon Festival	Diwali
When is it?		
What do people wear?		
What do people eat?		
What do people do?		

4 ▶1.19 Listen to Cannelle talking about an Irish festival called St Patrick's Day. Are the sentences right (✔) or wrong (✗)? Correct the sentences that are wrong.

1 Cannelle comes from Ireland.
2 St Patrick's Day is on 17th May.
3 The celebrations in Dublin are small.
4 You can hear Irish music on the streets.
5 You can go shopping on St Patrick's Day.
6 People wear blue hats on St Patrick's Day.
7 The fireworks are very popular.
8 People in the USA and Canada also celebrate St Patrick's Day.

5 Complete the paragraph about Carnaval in Rio de Janeiro with words from the box.

celebrate	decorate	dress up	festival	fireworks	masks	parades

My name is João Vitor and I come from Rio de Janeiro in Brazil. We have a very big and famous ¹............................ here called Carnaval. The date changes every year but it's usually at the end of February. We ²............................ Carnaval for four days. There are ³............................ through the streets, with music and dancing. People ⁴............................ in amazing clothes and wear ⁵............................ on their faces. They ⁶............................ the cities in bright colours. In the evenings, you can see ⁷............................ in the sky, and hear them too! It's a really exciting festival, not just for Brazilians like me but also for people around the world.

Project – Describe a festival

Work with a partner. Think of a festival you celebrate in your country. Talk together about the festival. Make notes about these things:
• the name of the festival
• when it is
• what people wear
• what people do
• what people eat

Write about your festival. Read your paragraph about the festival to the class.

3 Great sounds
I love listening to rap

VOCABULARY

1 ▶1.20 **Listen to the different types of music. Number them in the order you hear them.**

classical ☐   jazz ☐   pop ☐   rap ☐   rock ☐   soul ☐

▶1.21 **Now listen and check.**

2 Look at the picture. Where are Ravi, Jack and Molly?

3 A guitar is a musical instrument. Can you see one in the picture?

Find these musical instruments in the picture.

| keyboard   drums   violin   piano |

▶1.22 **Listen and check. Then repeat.**

About you

4 Ask and answer with a partner.
1 What's your favourite type of music?
2 When do you listen to music?
3 Where do you listen to music?
4 How often do you listen to music?
5 Do you listen to music alone or with friends?
6 Can you play any musical instruments? Which one(s)?

LISTENING

5 ▶1.23 **Listen to Ravi, Molly and Jack. Who can play …**

the drums? ....
the violin? ....
the piano? ....
the guitar? ....
the keyboard? ....

6 ▶1.23 **Listen again. Are the sentences right (✔) or wrong (✗)?**

0 Ravi liked the music lesson. ✔
1 Molly often listens to jazz at home.
2 Molly's favourite instrument is the violin.
3 Molly likes the drums.
4 Ravi doesn't like listening to the violin.
5 Jack hates rock music.

GRAMMAR   *like, don't like, hate, love + -ing*

7 **Put these sentences in the right place in the table.**

I quite like playing the piano.   *I hate listening to the drums.*   *I really love playing the piano.*

😊 ↓ ☹	a) .... *I love playing the keyboard.* *I like listening to jazz.* b) .... *I don't like listening to the violin.* c) ....

→ Grammar reference **page 145**

▶1.24 **Listen and check. Then repeat.**

8 **Look at each of the examples. How does the verb change from the simple to the *-ing* form?**

write → writing	run → running	help → helping	listen → listening

Now write the *-ing* form of these verbs in the correct columns.

choose   drive   get   learn   make   practise ride   sing   sit   swim   visit   win

⊙ Corpus challenge

Can you correct this sentence?
I like listen to rock music.

WRITING

9 **Write sentences about you and your family. Add your own ideas.**

I hate cooking pancakes but I really love eating them!
My brother doesn't like watching badminton but he quite likes playing it.

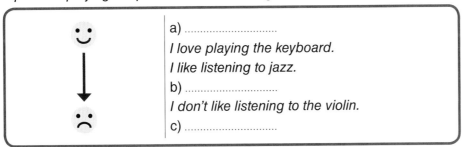

love	listen to	hip-hop
really like	watch	films
like	play	pancakes
quite like	do	running
don't like	go	badminton
hate	cook	homework

This is the MAD School

READING

1 Ravi is giving a PowerPoint presentation to his class about a music school. Read the PowerPoint slides quickly and answer the questions.

1 What is the name of the school?
2 What can you study there?

The MAD School: Music, Acting, Dance

The MAD School 1

- It's very different from our school.
- You don't pay to go there.
- It's for students between the ages of 14 and 19.

The MAD School 2

- You can learn about different kinds of music.
- You can study musical instruments.
- Some students record albums.

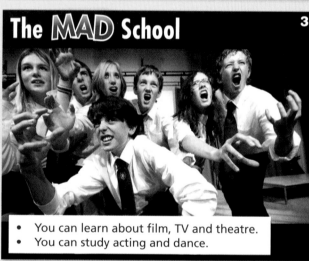

The MAD School 3

- You can learn about film, TV and theatre.
- You can study acting and dance.

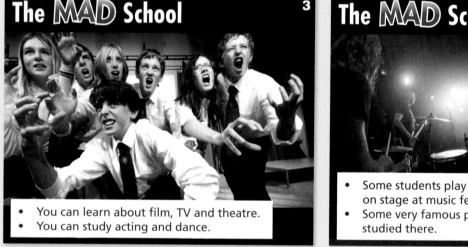

The MAD School 4

- Some students play and sing on stage at music festivals!
- Some very famous people studied there.

Thank you. Any questions?

2 Read the slides and comment again. Choose the right word(s) to complete the sentences.

0 The school teaches *music* / *cooking*.
1 It's *expensive* / *free* to go to the school.
2 The school is for *adults* / *teenagers*.
3 You can learn about *jazz* / *famous people*.
4 Students can make albums *at the school* / *at music festivals*.
5 Some famous people *were* / *teach* students at the school.
6 Ravi is ready to *ask* / *answer* some questions.

About you

3 Ask and answer with a partner.
1 Would you like to go to this school? Why? / Why not?
2 What would you like to study there?
3 What kind of school would you like to go to? Art/PE/Science School?
4 Do you have special schools like this in your country?

VOCABULARY

4 Complete the sentences with the words from the box in the correct form.

> become an actor   become famous
> ~~dance on stage~~   give a concert
> play in a band   record an album
> teach music

0 I have lots of fun at clubs but I really want to
.... *dance on stage* ....

1 My sister is a famous classical musician. She
.... in our town
every summer.

2 Amy loves going to the theatre
and watching plays. She wants to
....

3 Andy plays the drums well. He sometimes
.... with his friends
on Saturdays at the music club.

4 We've got ten new songs and they're really
good. Let's ....

5 I really want to ....
and be on TV and in lots of magazines.

6 My dad plays lots of instruments and he
.... at our school!

PRONUNCIATION Email addresses, phone numbers and names

For @ we say 'at'.
For . we say 'dot'.
For two numbers (77) we say 'double seven'.
For two letters (bb) we say 'double b'.

5 Practise with a partner.

1 Say this email address: *school@music.com*
2 Say this phone number: *0451 256 337*
3 Spell this name: *J-o-a-n-n-a*

▶1.25 Listen and check. Then repeat.

6 Work with a partner. Listen and write.

1 Say your email address.
2 Say your phone number.
3 Spell your grandfather or your grandmother's first name.

LISTENING

7 ▶1.26 Listen to the conversation. Write the information on the form.

> ### Music School Open Evening
> First name: **(1)** ....
> Family name: **(2)** ....
> Age: **(3)** ....
> Email address: **(4)** ....
> Phone number: **(5)** ....
> Open Evening on (day): **(6)** ....

SPEAKING

8 **Student A: You want to go to a dance school. Student B has information about a dance school.**
Student B: You want to go to a music school. Student A has information about a music school.

Make questions to ask your partner.

1 What / name / school?
2 Can / spell / please?
3 What / can / study / there?
4 How old / students?
5 What / email address?
6 What / phone number?

9 **Student A: Turn to page 129.**
Student B: Turn to page 130.

Now ask and answer the questions.

4 A true story
The missing ring

1993, Todd Henderson's graduation day

a

b I've got a present for you, Todd.

Wow, thanks, Mom. What a beautiful ring!

c Look, it's got your name inside as well – Todd Henderson.

I hope he looks after it!

d Two days later

e What are you doing Todd?

I'm looking for my ring. I can't find it!

Hi. Can you help me? I can't find my ring.

f What's it like? Can you describe it, please?

It's new, it's made of silver and it's got a big blue stone on it. It's got some writing on it too.

I'm sorry, sir. We don't have a ring like that here.

g Oh no, I think it's in the lake. What can I say to Mom?

READING

1 Read the story and answer the questions.

1 Why does Todd's mother give Todd a ring?
2 What happens to the ring?

2 Match the sentences to the pictures.

0 It's 1993 and Todd Henderson is 21. It's his last day at university.
  He and his friends are very happy. *picture a*
1 Todd asks the police about his ring. The news isn't good.
2 Todd's sure his ring is in the lake but he doesn't want to tell his mother.
3 Two days after he finishes university, Todd visits a lake. He wants to catch some fish.
4 On his graduation day, Todd's mother gives him a special ring. On the ring is the name of his university and the date of his graduation.
5 It's an expensive ring and Todd's mother doesn't want Todd to lose it.
6 Todd's ring isn't in his bedroom. He's very worried.

VOCABULARY   Describing things

3 ▶1.27 **Listen to and read the conversation between Todd and the police officer. Practise it with a partner.**

4 Match the pictures to the words.

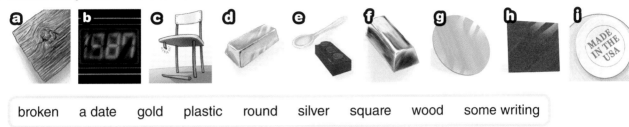

| broken | a date | gold | plastic | round | silver | square | wood | some writing |

▶1.28 **Listen and check. Then repeat.**

5 Complete the table with words from the conversation and Exercise 4. Think of some more describing words to complete each sentence.

Asking	Describing
What's it .... ? Can you .... it?	It's ....
	It's made of ....
	It's got .... on it.

6 Describe some things in your classroom.

A: *It's made of plastic. It's blue. It's got some numbers on it.*
B: *Is it a ruler?*
A: *Yes, it is.*

Corpus challenge

Can you see what's wrong with this sentence? Add one word.

I've got a new bed for my bedroom. It's of wood and it's not very large.

LISTENING

7 ▶1.29 **Listen to three people asking for things. Which thing are they looking for? Choose the right answer (A, B or C).**

Conversation 1

A    B    C

EP Get talking! → page 124

I'm afraid … (not) …
Oh, that's a pity.
What a shame.

SPEAKING

8 Draw a picture of a ring, key ring, earring or necklace. Describe it to your partner. Your partner tries to draw it.

Conversation 2

A    B    C

Conversation 3

A    B    C

How surprised were you?

READING

1 Read the second part of the story and answer the questions.

1 How old is Todd now?
2 Where is his ring now?

2 Look at these questions from journalists. Write Todd's answers.

0 Are you wearing the ring now?
   No, I'm not. It's in my drawer.
1 Were you surprised to get your ring back?
2 Where was your ring?
3 Can you describe the ring?
4 Was the ring a present?
5 How old were you in 1993?

3 What do you think of this story? Were you surprised by the ending?

GRAMMAR   *was / were*: + , − , ?

4 **Look at these examples from the story. Now choose the right word to complete the rules.**

The ring was inside the fish.
Journalists were very interested.
It wasn't in the lake.
Were you surprised?

> 1 The past simple of *be* with *it* is
> .... and with *you/they* is ....
> 2 To form the negative, we add ....

→ Grammar reference **page 146**

⊙ Corpus challenge

Can you correct this sentence?
The weather is good yesterday.

VOCABULARY   *how* + adjective

5 **Read some more questions about the story. Underline the adjectives in the questions.**

1 How <u>old</u> is the ring?
2 How expensive was it?
3 How big was the fish?
4 How difficult was it to find Todd?
5 How surprised was Todd?

a It wasn't very difficult.
b He was very surprised!
c It's 20 years old.
d It was quite big – 10 pounds.
e It was $200.

Read the rule below. Then match the questions and answers above.

> The answer to *how* + adjective can be *very*, *quite*, *not very* or a number.

PRONUNCIATION   Intonation in *How …* questions

6 ▶1.31 **Listen and repeat.**

1 How big is your school?
2 How old is your brother?
3 How late was the teacher?
4 How exciting was the film?
5 How difficult was the test?

About you

7 **Write questions with *how*. Answer the questions with a number or with *very / quite / not very*. Then ask and answer with a partner.**

0 funny / your best friend?
   How funny is your best friend?
1 tall / you?
2 good / you at English?
3 hot / the summers in your country?
4 clean / your hands?
5 long / your ring finger?
6 hungry / you?
7 tired / you today?
8 far / is it from your home to your school?

WRITING

Prepare to write—A description

GET READY Read the text and underline all the adjectives.

My favourite thing is my guitar. It was my mother's when she was a young girl. It's about 20 years old. It's quite big. It's made of light brown wood. I think it's very beautiful.

Complete the sentences with the adjectives.
1 It's a house. (big old)
2 I like my coat. (new green)
3 This is music! (fantastic)
4 There are some rings here. (expensive)
5 I've got a mobile phone. (very nice)

PLAN Make notes about your favourite thing. What is it? How old is it? What colour is it?

WRITE Write a paragraph of 30–40 words about your favourite thing.

IMPROVE Read your paragraph and your partner's. Check for mistakes with adjectives. Can you make your paragraph better?

Design and technology
Logos

1 Look at the four logos.

- Do you like them?
- What is each one for?

2 Read the text and answer the questions.

1 Which organisations are the logos for?
2 What do the organisations do?

LOGOS

A logo is a picture but it is a picture with meaning. Companies spend many thousands of pounds designing their logos. The best logos can cost even more.

The logo for Gap, the clothing company, is the name of the company in white on a dark blue background. In 2010, the company decided it was time to change their logo. But no one liked the new logo. So, after only a week, the company started to use their old logo again.

One of the logos for the social networking site Facebook does not use the whole word. It just uses the first letter. This letter is in white on a light blue background. Another Facebook logo has the whole word in white on a light blue background.

The Olympic Movement, who choose the city for the Olympic Games, use five coloured rings on a white background as their logo. The five rings link together. They represent the five parts of the world who compete in the Games: Africa, the Americas, Asia, Europe and Oceania.

The logo for the sports-clothing company Nike looks like a black check mark on a white background. Sometimes the logo has the word Nike above the check mark. But often now the company just use the check mark on its own.

3 Answer the questions.

1 Which company tried to change its logo in 2010?
2 Which companies have more than one logo?
3 Which companies have the name of the company on their logo or logos?
4 Which company usually uses the first letter of their name on its logo?
5 Which organisation never uses any letters or words on its logo?

4 Now think about the design of the logos. Which do you prefer?
Discuss each logo and talk about:

1 the use of capital letters or lower case
2 the shape of the background
3 the use of colour
4 the use of whole words or single letters
5 the use of images without words
6 the style of the writing (the font)

5 Look at the four Microsoft and Nestlé logos and their dates.

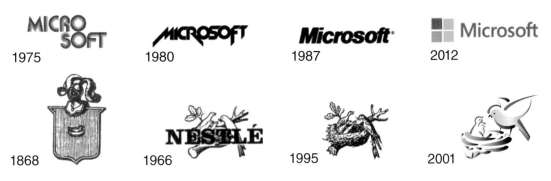

1975   1980   1987   2012

1868   1966   1995   2001

Discuss the logos. Include points
from Exercise 4.

1 Which logo in each set do you prefer?
2 How is each logo in the set different?
3 Can you think of a design for the
  company's next logo?

Project — Design a logo or make a logo collage

Choose one of these projects.
EITHER
Design a logo for your school or for a club.
• Think about each of the points in Exercise 4.
• Create your logo.
• Present and talk about your logo to the class.
OR
Work with a partner. Describe your day through logos.
• Does your breakfast cereal have a logo? Do your clothes have
  logos?
• Write a list. Find pictures of these logos on the internet and print
  them out.
• Make a collage of these logos to describe your day.
• Present and talk about your collage to the class.

Review 1
Units 1-4

VOCABULARY

1 Match the pictures to the words.

| cabbage | cereal | chilli | cucumber | honey | hot chocolate | mango | toast | yogurt |

0 *yogurt*

2 Put the words in the right group.

| ~~album~~ | bat | classical | competition | cream | curry | drums | goal | instrument |
| keyboard | lemon | match | oil | pop | racket | sauce | sugar | team |

Food	Music	Sport
	album	

3 Complete the word in each sentence.

0 Oh, no. My pen is **b**roken.............. . Can I borrow yours?

1 This beautiful bowl is made of **w**............................. .

2 He likes cooking **a**............................. . He doesn't like doing it with other people.

3 Can you **d**............................. your brother for me? Is he tall?

4 My new shoes were really **e**............................. – they were £100!

5 My homework book is in the **d**............................. of my desk.

6 It's his 13th birthday today. Now he's a **t**............................. .

7 My favourite breakfast is a bowl of **f**............................. fruit.

8 Keira Knightley is a really good **a**............................. . She is excellent in her new film.

GRAMMAR

4 ⊙ Choose the right word to complete the sentences.

1 I love *talk / talking* to my friend and I love *go / going* shopping with her too.

2 I have a lot of hobbies. I like singing. I *sing / am singing* in the school hall on Fridays.

3 How *old / age* is your sister?

4 In my free time, I *usually stay / stay usually* at home.

⊙ Correct the mistakes in these sentences.

5 I go often with my friends to the cinema.

6 How are you? I write to you to give you some news.

7 How size is your garden?

8 I like go to college because I like my teachers.

5 Put the words in the right order to make questions.

0 your brothers / what / wake up / do / time / usually / ?
What time do your brothers usually wake up?

1 cooking / what / you / are / ?

....

2 mum / the / does / play / guitar / your / ?

....

3 play / you / Tuesday / do / tennis / every / ?

....

4 your / you / at the moment / are / doing / homework / ?

....

5 your / brother / playing / this morning / football / is / ?

....

Now match the questions to the answers below. Then complete each answer with the verb in the correct tense.

a Yes, she .... (play) it really well. She .... (learn) a new song at the moment. It sounds great! ☐

b They ..*are sleeping*.. (sleep) at the moment but they usually .....*wake up*..... (wake up) at seven. [0]

c Yes, I am. I .... (do) my maths. It's really difficult! ☐

d No, he's out with his friends. They .... (watch) a film at Tom's house. ☐

e Yes, I do, and I often .... (play) on Saturdays as well. ☐

f I .... (cook) pasta. I usually .... (make) tomato sauce to go with it but today I .... (make) mushroom sauce. ☐

LISTENING

6 ▶1.32 Listen and complete the information.

SPORTS CENTRE

1 Sport:
....

2 Start time:
.... pm

3 Cost:
£.............................

4 First name:
....

5 Family name:
....

6 Phone number:
....

READING

7 Complete the five conversations. Choose A, B or C.

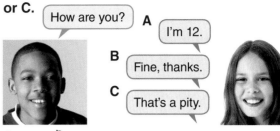

How are you?

A I'm 12.

B Fine, thanks.

C That's a pity.

Answer: B

1 What a great band!
   A Yeah, I like them too.
   B Here you are.
   C Not very often.

2 Is your necklace made of silver?
   A I'm wearing them.
   B I haven't got it.
   C I'm not sure.

3 That music's too loud!
   A I'm sorry, I'll turn it off.
   B That's a pity.
   C It's rock, I think.

4 How long is this film?
   A Not very much.
   B At four o'clock.
   C About two hours.

SPEAKING

8 Put the words in the right order to make questions.

1 name / your / what's / ?
2 you / where / live / do / ?
3 old / you / how / are / ?
4 favourite / what's / sport / your / ?

Ask and answer the questions with your partner. Take turns to speak.

9 Talk about your family. Take turns to speak.

Tell me about your family.

I've got two brothers …

5 Fantastic facts
Neil Armstrong walked on the moon

READING AND VOCABULARY

1 Look at the pictures and match them to the sentences in Exercise 2.

2 Do the quiz. Choose A, B or C.

1 Edmund Hillary and Tenzing Norgay climbed Mount Everest
   A on 9th January 1889.
   B on 7th August 1940.
   C on 29th May 1953.

2 Amelia Earhart crossed the Atlantic Ocean, alone, by plane
   A in 1918.   B in 1932.   C in 2005.

3 Leonardo da Vinci painted the *Mona Lisa*
   A in the 16th century.
   B in the 18th century.
   C in the 20th century.

4 Rafael Nadal played his first tennis match at Wimbledon
   A in 2003.   B in 2004.   C in 2005.

5 Neil Armstrong walked on the moon
   A on 4th July 1960.
   B on 21st July 1969.
   C on 3rd February 1973.

6 Shakira recorded her first album
   A in 1990.   B in 2000.   C in 2005.

7 Ada Lovelace completed the first computer program
   A in 1842.   B in 1942.   C in 1982.

8 Ringo Starr joined The Beatles
   A in April 1956.
   B in May 1960.
   C in September 1962.

9 Aristide Boucicaut opened the first department store in Paris
   A in 1752.   B in 1852.   C in 1952.

10 Neil Papworth texted the first text message
   A in January 1972.
   B in June 1984.
   C in December 1992.

▶ 1.33 Listen and check.

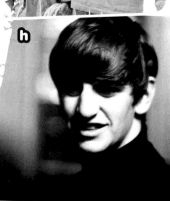

3 Test your partner.

> In 1990 …
>
> Shakira recorded her first album.

4 Look at the answers to the quiz again. Complete the rules for *in* and *on.*

> We use *in / on* for the date and the day, for example
> .... *9th January 1889,* .... *Tuesday.*
> We use *in / on* for months, years and centuries, for example
> .... *January,* .... *May 1960,* .... *2003,* .... *the 20th century.*

GRAMMAR   Past simple: regular verbs

5 Read these sentences.

> Andy Murray played his first match at Wimbledon in 2005.
> NASA's Curiosity Mars Rover landed on Mars on 6th August 2012.

→ Grammar reference **page 147**

Look at the verbs in the table. Write the past simple forms of the verbs
in the box below in the right column.

climb → climbed	change → changed	carry → carried	stay → stayed	clean → cleaned

cook	copy	enjoy	finish	help	invite	join	phone	play	study

6 Complete the sentences. Write the verb in the past simple.

Add *in* or *on* in sentences 5–8.

0 I .... *joined* .... (join) the school orchestra ....*in*.... February.

1 I .... (help) my sister with her homework yesterday.

2 He .... (phone) me last week.

3 My friend .... (copy) the answer.

4 I .... (practise) the piano yesterday evening.

5 My brother .... (cook) dinner .... Sunday.

6 My mum .... (study) history at university .... 1994.

7 My dad .... (play) for Manchester United .... September 1988.

8 She .... (invite) us to her birthday party .... 8th June.

> **⊙ Corpus challenge**
>
> **Can you correct the mistake here?**
> I went to London. In
> London, I ~~visit~~ a friend.
> I really enjoyed it.

PRONUNCIATION   Past simple verb endings

7 ▶ 1.34 Listen to three *-ed* sounds. Then
put the verbs in blue from Exercise 2 into
the correct column.

answered /d/	finished /t/	waited /ɪd/

▶ 1.35 Listen and check. Then repeat.

> **About you**
>
> **8** Make six sentences about you. Use the
> verbs in the box to help you.
> *We started school on 4th September.*
> *I visited China with my family in 2013.*
>
> | climb | complete | cross | dance |
> |---|---|---|---|
> | finish | join | open | paint | play |
> | record | travel | visit |
>
> Now say your sentences to your partner.

The Great Fire of London

VOCABULARY AND LISTENING

1 Match a–f in the picture to the words in the box.

> buildings   a crowded street   a fire   a rat   a sick person   wood

▶ 1.36 Listen and check. Then repeat.

2 Look at the four pictures a–d. What can you see?

3 ▶ 1.37 Listen and number the pictures 1–4.

4 ▶ 1.37 Listen again. Are the sentences right (✔) or wrong (✗)?

1 The Great Fire started in 1566.
2 London was bigger then than it is today.
3 Before the fire, houses were made of wood.
4 At that time, many people lived in boats on the River Thames.
5 St Paul's Cathedral is more than 300 years old.
6 The Great Fire of London started in the Monument.

a ☐

b ☐

c ☐

d ☐

READING

5 **Read the text. Choose the correct answer.**

Not many people died …
a) in the Great Fire.
b) of the Black Death.

The Great Fire and The Black Death

The Bad News!!
- The Black Death arrived in England in 1665.
- Rats carried the Black Death.
- People with the Black Death were very sick.
- Many thousands of people died.
- The Black Death was very bad in London.
- The Great Fire started in a bread shop on 2nd September 1666.
- Six people died in the fire.
- The Great Fire ended on 5th September 1666.
- After the fire, thousands of people didn't have anywhere to live.

The Good News!!
- The Great Fire killed the rats.
- The Great Fire stopped the Black Death.

6 **Read the text again. Write GF (Great Fire) or BD (Black Death).**

0 A lot of people died. *BD*
1 It started in 1666.
2 It lasted for a year.

3 It lasted for four days.
4 Rats carried it.
5 Rats died in it.

SPEAKING

7 **The Great Fire of London was an important event in British history.**
Think of an important event in the history of your country.
Talk about it with your partner. Use these questions to help you.
- What's the name of the event?
- When was the event?
- Where was the event?
- What were some of the things that happened?

8 **Tell the class about your event.**

Our important event from history is ....
It happened on (date) in (place).
These are some of the things that happened. There was … and then …

9 **Work in groups of six. Draw a time line and put your events on the time line.**

6 What a great job!
Where did you work?

READING AND VOCABULARY

1 Read the text. Which pictures show Nina and which show Julia?

2 Are the sentences right (✔) or wrong (✗)?

1 Nina and Julia are the same age.
2 Nina and Julia are at school this week.
3 Last week, Nina and Julia both worked nine hours a day.
4 Both Nina and Julia worked hard last week.
5 Nina liked her job more than Julia.

3 Read the text again and find these words. Then match them to sentences 1–6.

> boss   busy   customers   earn   office   staff

1 This means you're working hard and have lots to do.
2 These people buy things in shops or cafés.
3 When you have a job, this person tells you what to do.
4 These people work for a business.
5 There are usually desks, phones and computers in this place.
6 This means to get money for doing work.

STUDENTS AT WORK!

Nina and Julia are 14 years old and go to school in London. But they weren't at school last week – they were doing work experience. Of course, they didn't earn any money, and this week they are back in the classroom. But did they enjoy their week at work? What did they learn? We wanted to find out, so we asked them some questions.

WHERE DID YOU WORK?

NINA: I worked in a café.

JULIA: I worked for a TV company.

WHAT DID YOU DO?

NINA: I cleaned the tables and washed the floor and I also served the customers. I gave them their food and drinks and took the money. I started really early in the morning – at six o'clock! The café opened at seven o'clock and closed at six. I didn't stay until six o'clock – I finished work at two o'clock. The staff were friendly but we didn't have much time for talking. We were all really busy!

JULIA: I worked in the office of the TV company. I started at ten o'clock and finished at six o'clock. In the morning, I opened all the letters. Then I helped my boss with different jobs. Sometimes he told me to answer the phone. Other times he asked me to use the computer to look for information he needed. I was busy all day and sometimes I didn't stop for lunch!

DID YOU ENJOY IT?

NINA: No, I didn't! I wanted to work in a café because I like cooking. But I didn't do any cooking all week. I was very happy to go back to school.

JULIA: Yes, I did! At first I was worried, because I didn't want to work in the office. I wanted to work in the TV studio. But the staff were all very nice to me and I learned a lot about the business.

GRAMMAR Past simple: ?, –

4 Look at the examples in the table. Then read the text again and find more examples of past simple negatives and past simple questions.

Negatives	Questions	Short answers
They didn't earn any money.	What did they learn?	Yes, I did.
I didn't do any cooking.	Did you enjoy it?	No, I didn't.

→ Grammar reference **page 148**

5 Correct the sentences.

0 Nina worked for a TV company.
Nina didn't work for a TV company. She worked in a café.

1 The café opened at six o'clock in the morning.

2 Nina finished work at seven o'clock.

3 Julia opened the letters in the afternoon.

4 Julia used the computer to send emails.

5 Nina did the cooking in the café.

6 Julia worked in the TV studio.

Corpus challenge

Can you find and correct the mistake here?

Hi Maria. Do you see the football game? It was so cool. I hope you watched it.

LISTENING

6 ▶1.38 Listen to Joe talking about the job he did last week. Tick (✔) the correct picture (A, B or C).

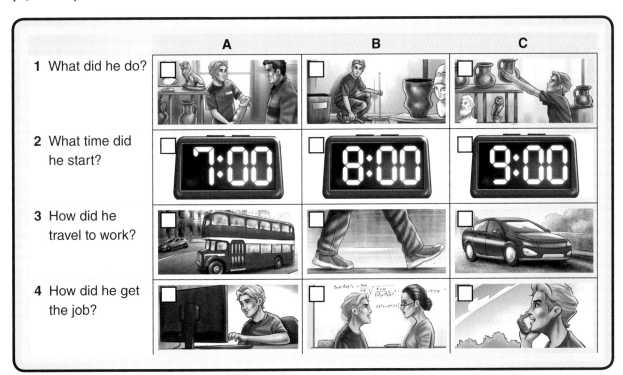

1 What did he do?

2 What time did he start?

3 How did he travel to work?

4 How did he get the job?

SPEAKING

7 ▶1.39 Listen and repeat.

8 Work with a partner. One of you is Joe and the other is Joe's friend. Use the table in Exercise 6 to make a conversation. Use the phrases from Exercise 7 in your conversation.

Where did you work?

I worked in the museum.

EP Get talking! → page 125

That's brilliant!
Congratulations!
Wow!
Oh no! That sounds boring.
Really?

50 different jobs!

READING AND VOCABULARY

1 **Read the article about Daniel Seddiqui and answer the questions.**

1 What did Daniel do?
2 Why did he do it?
3 Did he enjoy it?

2 **Look at the map of Daniel's trip and the list of jobs. Match each job to a picture on the map.**

▶1.42 **Listen and repeat.**

3 **Read again and choose the correct answer, A or B.**

1 How did Daniel travel from job to job?
  A by plane   **B** by car
2 Where did he usually stay?
  A in hotels   **B** in people's homes
3 What did Daniel do in Nebraska?
  A He worked as a farmer.   **B** He worked as a cook.
4 Where did he work as a model?
  A in North Carolina   **B** in Florida
5 How did he feel about working as a photographer?
  A He hated it.   **B** He enjoyed it.

4 **Which of Daniel's jobs would you like to do?**

---

50 weeks, 50 states, 50 different jobs

When Daniel Seddiqui was 26, he travelled around America for a year. He visited all 50 states and worked for a week in each one. He didn't use buses or planes – he travelled by car from job to job. He earned money for every job he did but hotels were too expensive for him. He usually stayed in his boss's home, or with one of the other workers. 'People were very good to me,' says Daniel. 'They looked after me really well.'

But why did Daniel do this? 'I wanted to travel and learn about my country,' he says. 'And I wanted to try lots of different jobs.' Things weren't always easy for Daniel. In week 7, he worked as a farmer in Nebraska. 'The days were long and I got really dirty,' he says. In week 38, he was a cook in a fish restaurant in Maryland. 'That was really hard! Often I didn't even have time to get a drink of water.' Other jobs were fun. He worked in a theme park in Florida and as a model in North Carolina. In Alaska, he was a photographer. 'That was great. Alaska is a very beautiful place,' says Daniel.

Some of Daniel's jobs

- factory worker
- farmer
- engineer
- car mechanic
- TV weather man
- football coach
- model
- fisherman

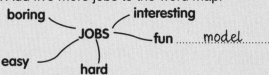

5 Copy the word map into your notebook. Complete it with jobs from Exercise 2. Add five more jobs to the word map.

boring — interesting

JOBS — fun ....*model*........

easy — hard

6 Work in groups. Compare your word maps and talk about what jobs you want to do when you're older.

> I want to be an engineer when I'm older.

> Do you? I don't. I want to be an actor.

PRONUNCIATION   Word stress

7 ▶1.43 **Listen and repeat the words. Put them into the right column.**

~~company~~   customer   difficult   ~~engineer~~   expensive
magazine   mechanic   museum   understand

Ooo	oOo	ooO
company		*engineer*

WRITING

GET READY Look at the text about Daniel. Find examples of full stops (.), capital letters (A, B …) and apostrophes (').

Full stops – These are at the end of a sentence.
Capital letters – Use these after a full stop; for names, days of the week and months; for the word 'I'.
Apostrophes – These are for contractions (*I've got*) and for possessives (*Jane's dog*).

Read Daniel's blog for week 9 and add full stops, capital letters and apostrophes.

Week 9
i didnt have much free time this weekend on saturday afternoon i started my new job as a shop assistant its in a town called fishtail in montana the shop belongs to a man called bill i cleaned the floors in the shop and served customers then on sunday i cooked soup i was really busy but i enjoyed working in bills shop

PLAN Make notes about what you did last weekend.

WRITE Write a blog of about 50 words about your weekend.

IMPROVE Read your blog and your partner's. Check for mistakes with punctuation.

Culture
Teens at work

1 Discuss these questions in groups.

- Do you have a part-time job after school or at weekends?
- Would you like to work after school or at the weekend? Why? / Why not?
- What kind of job would you like to have?

2 Read the three messages quickly. <u>Underline</u>:

- each student's name
- each student's age
- the job they do
- the country they come from

Blogspot > Teen life

Work

I really want to work but in my country young people can't work until the age of 15. It's illegal! So I can't get a part-time job because I'm only 14. Lots of my friends are 15 and have got part-time jobs. When we go out, they've got money to buy clothes. Some of them even save their money and then buy new phones and computers! Sure, my parents give me pocket money but it's just not fair. I want to work!

Jewel. Johannesburg.

Hey Jewel, that's tough that you can't do part-time work! Things here in Canada are very different from South Africa. I'm the same age as you and I work in a bread shop on the weekend. I put the bread on the shelves and help the customers. I mostly work on Saturdays, for four hours. Sometimes I work Sundays too when they need me. The money's not too bad and I can save for things. It's legal here for 12–14-year-olds to work eight hours at weekends and two hours after school!!

Carter. Calgary.

Hi guys. I read your posts. I'm younger than you two – I'm only 13 – but I work every weekend and it's legal! I live in New Zealand on a farm with my family. At weekends, I help my mum and dad on the farm. And they pay me! When I take food to the sheep, I drive the tractor. It's cool! Kids on farms here can drive tractors when they're 12! Luckily I don't get up when my dad does – at five in the morning. Kids here can't work until after six o'clock!

Lucas. Masterton.

3 Read the messages again and answer the questions.

1 What do Jewel's friends spend their money on?
2 What do Jewel's parents give her every week?
3 What does Carter do in the bread shop?
4 What does Carter do with the money he earns?
5 When does Lucas work?
6 What does Lucas do on the tractor?

4 Read the three messages again. Put R (right), W (wrong), or DS (doesn't say)
for each country.

	South Africa	Canada	New Zealand
It is legal for children under 15 to work.			
It is legal for 14-year-olds to work eight hours at the weekend.			
It is illegal for children to work before 6 am.			
It is legal for 13-year-olds to drive tractors.			

5 Find out answers to these questions. Use the internet.

1 Can teenagers work in your country? At what age?
2 How many hours they can work?
3 What kinds of jobs can teenagers do?
4 What kinds of jobs can't they do?

6 Write a short text to post on the blogspot using the information from Exercise 5.

7 ▶1.44 Listen to Sharon talking to her grandfather, Paul. She's asking him
about the jobs he did when he was at school. How much did he earn every week?

8 ▶1.44 Listen again. Are the sentences right (✔) or wrong (✗)?

1 Sharon is 12 years old.
2 Paul was a teenager in the 1960s.
3 None of Paul's friends had jobs.
4 A paper boy collects old newspapers for recycling.
5 Paul got up every day at five o'clock.
6 Paul finished work at eight-thirty.
7 Paul did his paper round every morning.

Project — Interview someone

Interview one of your grandparents, or an older person that you know.
Find out the answers to these questions.

• What jobs did they do when they were teenagers?
• What did they do at work?
• How much did they earn?
• How many of their friends worked?

1 Prepare a questionnaire.
2 Interview the person.
3 Make notes.
4 Give a mini-presentation to the class.

7 Going places
We went to Turkey on holiday

VOCABULARY AND LISTENING

1 Look at the pictures. Match the activities to the words in the box.

buy presents	ride a bike
go camping	stay at a hotel
go sightseeing	swim
go to the beach	take photos

About you

2 What do you do when you're on holiday? Talk to your partner.

3 ▶1.45 Listen to Jack and Molly talking about their holidays. Answer the questions.

1 Where did Molly go?
2 Where did Jack go?
3 Did they enjoy their holidays?

4 ▶1.45 Listen again and look at the pictures. What activities did Jack and Molly do? Write J or M next to each picture.

GRAMMAR Past simple: irregular verbs

5 Look at the sentences from Jack and Molly's conversation. Match the irregular past simple forms to the correct verb.

1 My friend Annabel *came* with us.
2 We *swam* in the sea every day.
3 We *rode* our bikes.
4 We *got up* late every day.
5 We *had* a great time.
6 My parents *gave* me a new camera.
7 I *took* hundreds of pictures.
8 I *went* to Istanbul, in Turkey.
9 I *saw* some interesting places.
10 I *bought* you a present.
11 I only *ate* one sweet.
12 We *could* walk to the beach in five minutes.

buy
can
come
eat
get up
give
go
have
ride
see
swim
take

▶1.46 Listen and check. Then repeat.

→ Grammar reference page 149

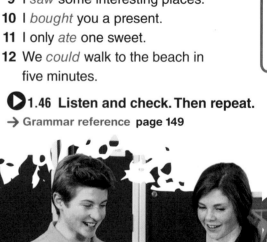

6 1.47 **Close your book and listen. You will hear the irregular past tense. Say the verb.**

7 **Complete Jack and Molly's conversation. Use the words and phrases in the box.**

> Did   Did   didn't   get up   Of course not
> take   Yes, I did

Jack: How was your summer holiday, Molly?
Molly: It was brilliant! I .... want to leave!
Jack: .... you .... early every day?
Molly: .... ! We got up late and we went to bed late.
Jack: .... you .... any photos?
Molly: .... I took hundreds of them!

8 **Make conversations. Use the verb in brackets and a short answer.**

1 (go)
.... you .... to the mountains for your holiday?
No, we .... We .... to the beach.

2 (swim)
.... you .... in the sea every day?
Yes, we .... , and we also .... in the pool.

3 (buy)
.... you .... any clothes?
No, of .... ! But I .... a lot of presents.

4 (eat)
.... you .... a lot of ice cream?
Yes, of .... ! And we .... a lot of sweets.

5 (have)
.... you .... a good time?
Of .... ! We .... a great time.

9 **Write three new holiday conversations.**

> **Corpus challenge**
>
> **Can you see what's wrong with this sentence?**
> My family and friends were there and they gived me a lot of presents.

> **EP Get talking!** → page 125
>
> Of course not!
> I don't think so.
> Oh no, I hate …

READING AND WRITING

10 **Complete the email from Ravi to Molly and Jack. Use the verbs in the box in the correct form.**

> ~~be~~   buy   can   eat   go   have   love
> see   stay   take   visit

> **To:** Molly and Jack
> **From:** Ravi
>
> Hi guys! I hope your holidays
> **(0)** .... were .... good.
> I **(1)** .... a great time in New York. It was a special holiday for my dad's 50th birthday. We **(2)** .... at a nice hotel called Alberto's. We **(3)** .... see lots of famous places from our bedroom window. The food in New York was great. We **(4)** .... in a different restaurant every night. My favourite was Chinese food. We did lots of sightseeing and **(5)** .... some interesting museums. We **(6)** .... to the Statue of Liberty and the Empire State Building. We also **(7)** .... a show on Broadway. Of course, my mum **(8)** .... the department stores. She **(9)** .... new clothes for all of us. I **(10)** .... lots of photos. They're all online now – have a look!
>
> **Download attachment**
>
>

11 **Write a message to a friend about your holiday. Make notes first.**

- Where did you go?
- What did you do?
- What did you see?
- What did you eat?

READING AND VOCABULARY

1 Read the paragraph about scouts and look at the pictures. Answer the questions in groups.

1 What do scouts do?
2 How many scouts are there in the world?
3 What is the 'Jamboree'?
4 Are *you* a scout? If not, would you like to be one?

Scouts

Scouts are girls and boys between six and 25 years old. They do lots of different activities, including camping, cooking and sports. Around 28 million young people, across 200 countries, are scouts. Every few years, scouts from around the world get together to meet each other and have fun. This is called the 'Jamboree'.

A very long bike ride

One year, two Australian scouts, Adam and Stephen, decided to cycle to the scout Jamboree. It was in Sweden, about 20,000 km from their home in Adelaide! They didn't take normal bikes, they took bikes with three wheels and seats instead. These are more comfortable and easier to ride up hills.

They packed everything they needed on their bikes. They had a tent each, things to cook with, clothes, maps, computers and phones, and things to repair the bikes. They also needed passports because they planned to travel through 22 different countries.

The journey began in Australia but it didn't go well. After just a few days, Adam's bike broke. He left Stephen and travelled home by coach. He got a new wheel for

his bike, then bought a plane ticket and flew to Perth. From the airport, he caught a train to a town called Merridien. He put his bike together on the station platform and cycled to meet Stephen.

After that, they flew to Johannesburg and then they began their bike ride through Africa. They slept in tents by the road, and in some places they saw a lot of wild animals. One night, they could hear lions, and another night, an elephant walked past their tents.

In Europe, they saw snow for the first time in their lives and rode up some very high mountains. In every country along the way, they visited scout groups and talked about their journey. They met a lot of interesting people and had lots of adventures. The journey took 269 days.

2 Read the text about two scouts and their journey. Answer the questions.

1 How far is Sweden from Australia?
2 What did the boys pack to take with them?
3 Did they have any problems on the journey?
4 What kind of animals did they see in Africa?
5 What did they do in Europe?
6 How long did the journey take?

Do you know about any other long journeys?
Would you like to do a journey like this?

3 Read the text again. Match the words in blue to the pictures.

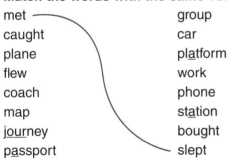

4 Look at the irregular past tenses in purple in the text. Write the verbs.

PRONUNCIATION Sounds and spelling

5 Match the words with the same vowel sound.

met	group
caught	car
plane	pla<u>t</u>form
flew	work
coach	phone
map	sta<u>t</u>ion
<u>jou</u>rney	bought
p<u>a</u>ssport	slept

▶ 1.49 Listen and check.

LISTENING

6 ▶ 1.50 Listen to Marion talking about a journey. How did she travel? Number the pictures in order. There's one picture you don't need.

SPEAKING

7 Tell your partner a travel story. Include this information in your story:

• When you went
• Where you went
• Who you went with
• How you travelled
• How long your journey took

Useful words
This happened … months/years ago.
First we …
Then we …
We took a … / We caught a … / We went by bus/car.
Anyway …

a ☐ b ☐ c ☐ d ☐ e ☐

8 Special places
Roald Dahl's room

VOCABULARY AND READING

1 Look at the pictures and discuss the questions.

- Which of these books do you know? Which do you like best?
- Who wrote the books?
- Can you remember any of the stories?
- What are your favourite books?

2 Look at the picture of Roald Dahl's room and find these things.

armchair   blanket   carpet   cupboard   drawer
drawings   lamp   photographs   shelf

▶ 1.51 **Listen and check. Then repeat.**

3 What do you think Roald Dahl used this room for? Read the article quickly to check.

Roald Dahl's Special Place

Roald Dahl's room was inside a hut, a small building in his garden. No one went inside his hut. It was his own place.

It was a small room and Roald Dahl did not keep it very tidy. But all he needed was somewhere to write! He sat in an old armchair and used a board across his knees as his writing desk. There was a big old table with drawers in the room. But he did not use this as a desk. Instead, he kept scissors, photos and other things on it – and of course a lot of pencils. He always wrote in pencil. An old metal cupboard stood in the corner of the room with papers and other things inside.

On the walls, there were drawings, photos of his family and letters from his fans.

When it was cold in the winter, he put a blanket over his legs to keep warm. He didn't need anything else.

It's quite hard to believe that Roald Dahl wrote so many of his famous books in this small room!

4 **Find the past simple of these verbs in the article.**

be   go   keep   put   sit   stand   use   write

5 **Read the article again. Answer the questions.**

1 Where was Roald Dahl's writing room?
2 Who else went into his room?
3 Where did he sit and write?
4 What did he keep on the old table?
5 Why did he have so many pencils?
6 How did he keep warm when it was cold?

GRAMMAR   *someone, anyone,* etc.

6 **Look at the table. Match 1–3 to a–c.**

1	someone anyone no one	These words are about … **a)** a place.
2	somewhere anywhere	**b)** a thing.
3	something anything nothing	**c)** a person.

→ Grammar reference **page 150**

7 **Find three sentences in the article with words from the table.**

1 ....
....
2 ....
....
3 ....
....

8 **Complete the pronouns with *-thing, -one* or *-where*.**

0 Did any*one* .... come to your party?
1 Some .... gave me these shoes. Do you like them?
2 There wasn't any .... in the drawer. I looked.
3 Can you think of any .... to go this afternoon?
4 I'm hungry but there's no .... in the fridge!
5 She went some .... hot for her holidays.
6 No .... told me that you wrote stories!
7 I'd like some .... to eat, please.

9 **Complete the sentences with *something, anything* or *nothing*.**

0 Can you bring .....*something*..... to tomorrow's class, please?
1 Do you remember .... about the film?
2 I looked in the drawer this morning. It's empty. There's .... there.
3 It's very dark. I can't see ....
4 I learn .... new in English every day.

Corpus challenge

Can you correct this sentence?
I don't have ~~nothing~~ to do on Friday night.

PRONUNCIATION   /ɜ:/ and /ɔ:/

10 ▶1.52 **Listen to the sounds /ɜ:/ and /ɔ:/. Look at the words and think about the sounds. Put the words into the right column.**

corner   drawer   first   floor   journey
saw   wall   warm   were   work   world

bird /ɜ:/	board /ɔ:/

▶1.53 **Listen and check. Then repeat.**

About you

11 What does your room look like? What have you got in it? Is it tidy or untidy?

Write some notes about your room.

Now tell your partner what your room is like.

My special place is the beach

LISTENING AND VOCABULARY

1 Roald Dahl liked writing stories in his room. It was his special place. What other things do people like doing in their 'special places'? Match the verbs in box A to the words in box B. There are more than six answers!

A
> draw   listen to   paint   play   read   write

B
> computer games   a diary   the drums
> the guitar   magazines   music   pictures
> songs   the sound of the wind/sea   stories

2 ▶1.54 Listen to three teenagers, Gary, Alison and Jo, talking about their special places.

Look at the pictures. Match the teenagers to their special places. Write the letters in column 1.

Gary

Alison

Jo

a

b

c

	1 place	2 What they like doing there
Gary		
Alison		
Jo		

3 ▶1.54 Listen again. What do they like doing in their special places? Write the answers in column 2.

READING

4 Put sentences a–d in the right order to make a short conversation.

a I'd love to. What time's the film?
b OK. Let's meet there half an hour before.
c Would you like to go to the cinema this evening?
d It starts at 7.30.

5 Look at the conversation in Exercise 4 and discuss the answers to these questions with your partner.

How did you decide …
- the first line of the conversation?
- the second line of the conversation?
- the third line of the conversation?
- the last line of the conversation?

6 **Jo wants to play music with her friend, Chris.**
Complete the conversation. What does Chris say to Jo?
Write the correct letter A–G in each space. There are two letters that you don't need.

Jo: What are you doing this evening, Chris?

Chris: 0 D ....

Jo: Would you like to come round to my house and play music?

Chris: 1 ....

Jo: That's OK. I need to help cook the dinner!

Chris: 2 ....

Jo: Perfect! I wrote a new song yesterday. We can try and play it.

Chris: 3 ....

Jo: No. Can you help me do that this evening?

Chris: 4 ....

Jo: Great! See you later.

A So, shall I come later, at 8 o'clock, then?

B Let's ask my brother.

C Wow, that's great. Did you write words for it as well?

D Nothing special. Why?

E What do you want to do?

F Of course! Then we can play and sing!

G I'd love to. But I've got to do my homework first.

SPEAKING

7 **Have a conversation with your partner.**

Make plans for this evening. Use these expressions from Exercise 4 and 6 to help you plan what to say.

What are you doing this evening?
Would you like to come round to my home and … ?
Shall I bring … ?
Let's ask …
Can you bring … ?
What do you want to do?

Maybe we can …
Nothing special.
I'd love to.
Yes, but I've got to …
That's OK. I have to …
I'm sure we can.
Great. See you later.

WRITING

Prepare to write – A description of a special place

GET READY Read about Tom's special place.

• Where is it?
• What does he like to do there?

Read the text again and underline *because* and *so*.
Think about how they join the two parts of the sentence.

Now join these sentences using *so* or *because*.

1 I'm wearing my coat .... it's very cold.
2 The bus didn't come on time, ... we were late for school.
3 I was tired, ... I went to bed.
4 Sorry, I can't come this evening .... I've got lots of homework.

PLAN Make notes about your special place.

• Where is it?
• Why is it special for you?
• What do you like to do there?

WRITE Write a paragraph of 40–60 words about your special place. Include *because* and *so* in your writing.

CHECK Read your paragraph and your partner's. Talk about how to make your descriptions better. Then rewrite your paragraph.

My special place is the beach. I like to go there in the mornings because there's no one else there. I like to feel the sand on my feet, so I take off my shoes and walk along the beach. All I can hear is the sound of the birds and the sound of the sea. I love it!

History
The history of flight

a

b

c

d

e

Flying machines

For many centuries, people thought humans could fly like the birds. The famous artist Leonardo da Vinci believed this when he studied flight in the 1480s. He designed many 'ornithopters' – machines with wings that go up and down like a bird's. We now know that humans cannot fly like this.

Two brothers, Joseph and Jacques Montgolfier, made the world's first hot-air balloons. They did this by making a fire under a silk bag so it filled with hot air. Their first passengers were a sheep, a chicken and a duck. Later that year, 1783, they sent the first ever humans on a flight.

Between 1799 and 1850, an Englishman called George Cayley designed many gliders. One of them had a box under the wings, like a boat with wheels. Some people say a ten-year-old boy flew in this for a few metres. George Cayley never flew in his gliders.

In the 1890s, a German engineer, Otto Lilienthal, improved gliders even more. After more than 2,500 flights, Otto Lilienthal died in an accident when he was flying one of his gliders.

In 1900, two brothers, Orville and Wilbur Wright, from Ohio, USA, began to study the work of George Cayley and Otto Lilienthal. First they built their own glider. Then, in 1902, they started designing an engine for it.

On 17th December 1903, Orville Wright flew their plane, The Flyer, for the first time. The flight lasted 12 seconds, and the plane travelled about 36.5 metres. Then, in 1905, Wilbur flew for 38 km. He only stopped because he had no more fuel. Humans were finally able to fly! Planes improved a lot in the 20th century and are now a part of all our lives.

1 What do you know about the history of flight? What would you like to know?

2 Look at the pictures. With a partner, put the flying machines in order from first to last.

3 Read the text quickly and check your answer to Exercise 2.

4 Read the text again. Find these things in the pictures.

balloon   glider   plane   tail   wheel   wing

Which of these does not have an engine?

a) glider   **b)** plane

5 Match the names to the pictures.

George Cayley   Leonardo da Vinci   The Montgolfier brothers
Otto Lilienthal   The Wright brothers

6 Match the dates to the way we say them.

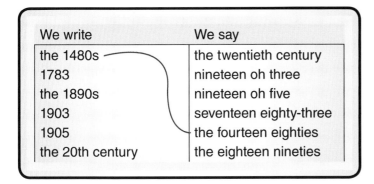

We write	We say
the 1480s	the twentieth century
1783	nineteen oh three
the 1890s	nineteen oh five
1903	seventeen eighty-three
1905	the fourteen eighties
the 20th century	the eighteen nineties

Find the dates in the text. Why are they important?

In the 1480s, Leonardo da Vinci began to study flight.

7 Work in pairs. Student A: Read the first three paragraphs of the text and answer questions 1–5.

1 What kind of flying machines did Leonardo da Vinci design?
2 How did the Montgolfier brothers make their balloons fly?
3 Which animals travelled on the first balloon flight?
4 What did George Cayley design?
5 How far did the ten-year-old boy fly?

Student B: Read the last three paragraphs and answer questions 6–10.

6 How did Otto Lilienthal die?
7 Where did Orville and Wilbur Wright come from?
8 What did they begin doing in 1902?
9 How many seconds did their first flight take?
10 Why did Wilbur stop his flight in 1905?

With your partner, ask and answer each other's questions.

Project **Make and fly a paper glider**

Turn to page 131 and make the glider. Fly your glider. Then answer these questions.
1 How far did your glider fly?
2 How many seconds did it fly for?

Review 2
Units 5–8

VOCABULARY

1 Choose the right word to complete the sentences.

0 Their plane arrived at the *platform* / ⟨airport⟩ at ten thirty.

1 It's dark in here. Can you turn on the *lamp* / *shelf*?

2 There are a lot of *customers* / *bosses* in the shop today. It's very busy!

3 My dad's a *mechanic* / *farmer*. He keeps sheep and cows.

4 That's better. That chair was hard. This one's really *tidy* / *comfortable*.

5 I keep my *diary* / *passport* in my bag. I like to write in it every day.

6 It's very cold in here. Can you lend me a *carpet* / *blanket*?

7 William's brother is a famous artist. He does amazing *drawings* / *drawers*.

8 We usually travel to London by *staff* / *coach*. It's cheaper than the train.

2 Match the verbs and the nouns.

1 open	a a picture
2 cross	b a project
3 join	c a restaurant
4 climb	d a club
5 play	e a match
6 paint	f a river
7 complete	g a tree

3 Match the words in the box to sentences 1–10.

> blanket   building   century   cook
> cupboard   ~~department store~~   office
> rat   scissors   sightseeing   sweet

0 You can buy lots of different things here. *department store*

1 You can keep things in here.

2 This is a small animal.

3 You can do this on holiday.

4 Your school and your house are examples of this.

5 People work in this place.

6 This is a job.

7 You can eat this.

8 You can cut with these.

9 This keeps you warm.

10 This means 'one hundred years'.

GRAMMAR

4 ◉ Choose the right word to complete the sentences.

1 My birthday party was great. There *was* / *were* a lot of people there.

2 I went with my friends to the mountains and we *climb* / *climbed* the hill.

3 Yesterday was my birthday and I *had* / *got* a computer.

4 Please, can you bring *something* / *anything* to the picnic?

◉ Correct the mistakes in these sentences.

5 Last summer I went to the United States. Some days it was hot but on others it rain.

6 Today we watched a football game but my sister don't like it very much.

7 At my party, I danced, singed and ate and drank a lot of things.

8 I didn't do nothing special.

5 Write the past simple of each of these verbs.

0 come	*came*			
1 begin	....	6 meet	....
2 buy	....	7 sleep	....
3 catch	....	8 swim	....
4 fly	....	9 ride	....
5 give	....	10 take	....

6 **Make sentences or questions about the past.**

0 They / come / yesterday?
Did they come yesterday?
1 I / not / see / that film / last night.
2 They / can / cycle / 50 km / in a day.
3 You / get / an email / this morning?
4 She / not / sleep / in a tent / on her holiday.
5 They / clean / their classroom / last week?
6 He / travel / to India / last winter.
7 We / not / stay / in a hotel / in London.
8 She / have / a computer / in her room?

READING

7 **Which notice (A–F) says this (1–4)? For questions 1–4, choose the correct letter A–F.**

0 This is closed one day a week. B
1 People can buy things to read or play with here.
2 It is not possible to visit this place today.
3 You can go here to have your sandwiches.
4 You should not eat in this place.

A
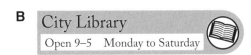
SPORTS CENTRE
Do not take food into the pool area

B

City Library
Open 9–5   Monday to Saturday

C

Palace Museum
Picnic tables for visitors in garden

D

GARLAND ZOO
Sorry, elephant house closed until tomorrow

E
Castle tours –
only £3.00 today!
Please wait here. Next tour begins at 2 pm.

F
Museum
SHOP
We sell books, toys and more

8 ▶ 1.55 **Listen and choose the right answers.**

1 The walls in the room were
A blue.
B green.
C yellow.

2 There were photographs of the writer's family
A on the walls.
B on the shelves.
C on the table.

3 The writer's new book is about
A Africa.
B elephants.
C lions.

4 The writer's first book is called
A *Leaving Home.*
B *Travelling Time.*
C *Travelling Home.*

5 The writer is
A 20 years old.
B 30 years old.
C 50 years old.

SPEAKING

9 **Put the words in the right order to make questions.**

1 live / you / flat / house / or / a / do / in / a / ?
2 rooms / how / there / many / are / ?
3 you / any / got / brothers / sisters / and / have / ?
4 big / bedroom / or / your / is / small / ?

Ask and answer the questions with your partner. Take turns to speak.

10 **Now talk about your room. Take turns to speak.**

Tell me about your room.

The walls are white and the carpet is blue. There are some shelves with …

9 Clothes and fashion
Those shoes are yours

VOCABULARY

1 Match the clothes a–h in the picture to the words in the box.

> cap   jacket   jumper   shorts
> socks   swimming costume

▶ 1.56 Listen and check. Then repeat.

2 Which clothes are:

yellow?   orange?   pink and white?
black?   red?   black and purple?
light green?   dark blue?
The jumper is yellow.

LISTENING AND READING

3 ▶ 1.57 Listen and answer.

1 What colour are Nick's socks?
2 Who likes the colour orange?

Mina: I think our clothes are dry now. Whose shorts are these?
Anita: They're mine.
Mina: And these pink and white socks? Are they yours as well, Anita?
Eddie: No, the pink and white socks are Nick's.
Mina: Right. They're very pretty, Nick.
Nick: My mum gave them to me!
Mina: Sorry! Whose jumper is this?
Eddie: It's mine. Thanks.
Mina: And this is my baseball cap. The light green one.
Anita: Isn't that green cap yours, Eddie?
Nick: No, the green cap's hers and the black cap's his.
Eddie: Yeah, that's right. The black cap's mine.
Mina: Is this dark blue jacket yours, Nick?

Nick: Has it got lots of pockets?
Mina: Yes.
Nick: Then it's my jacket.
Eddie: Whose swimming costume is that?
Mina: That's my costume. Orange is my favourite colour! Whose socks are these? The black and purple ones. Are they yours, too, Nick?
Nick: No, they're hers!
Anita: Yes, they're my socks. And I think they're very nice, thank you!

OK, so these clothes here are ours and those clothes are theirs. Let's put them in our tent before it rains!

4 Read the conversation in Exercise 3 and match
the clothes a–h to the people.

a The pink and white socks are Nick's.

▶1.58 **Then listen and check.**

5 Ask and answer about the clothes.

A: *Whose pink and white socks are these?*
B: *They're Nick's.*
A: *Whose black baseball cap is this?*
B: *It's Eddie's.*

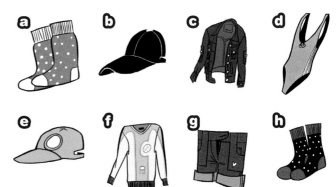

GRAMMAR Pronouns and determiners

6 Complete the sentences with the pronouns in the box.

hers	his	~~mine~~	ours	theirs	yours	yours

Determiners			Pronouns	
It's	my	jacket.	It's	.........mine.......... .
Are they	your	shorts?	Are they	............................?
It's	her	swimming costume.	The swimming costume's	....
It's	his	jumper.	The jumper's	....
They're	our	socks.	The socks are	....
They're	your	caps.	The caps are	....
They're	their	clothes.	These clothes are	....

→ Grammar reference **page 151**

Can you you find all the pronouns on page 58?

7 Complete the sentences with pronouns.

0 Students, here are your tickets for the school play. Jack and Molly, these are ....*yours*.......... .

1 I keep a diary every year. All these diaries are ....

2 My brother's got hundreds of old magazines. Those magazines are all ....

3 We live in that house. It's ....

4 You have so many clothes! Are all these .... ?

5 She painted that picture. That picture is ....

6 Sue and Mike are dentists. Those white coats are ....

8 Practise the conversation from Exercise 3
in groups of four.

Corpus challenge

Can you see what's wrong with this sentence?

I bought a short skirt because mine is very long and a pair of jeans because mines are broken.

SPEAKING

9 Tina is getting ready for a beach holiday.
Brad is getting ready for a skiing holiday.
Which things are Tina's?
Which things are Brad's?

dress	jumper	shorts	sun hat
sunglassses	swimming costume		
thick socks	towel	trousers	
warm hat	warm jacket		

I think the sun hat is hers and the warm hat is his.

Is your jumper made of cheese?

READING AND VOCABULARY

About you

1 What are your clothes and shoes made of?

cotton   wool   leather   plastic

My jeans and my socks are made of cotton, my shoes are made of leather and my jumper is made of wool.

2 Look at the pictures. What do you think these things are made of?

3 Read the article and check your ideas.

They're made of ... *what?*

Are you wearing a pair of leather shoes? Is your jumper made of wool? Sorry, that's not cool! You need to wear clothes made of something else. Are you ready to be surprised? Then read on.

- A group of fashion students from Bath in the UK made five amazing dresses and they were all made of cheese. Great for cold weather but perhaps not so good in the summer!
- Cork comes from trees and we sometimes find it in the top of bottles. But did you know you can also use cork to make clothes, handbags and shoes? It's very popular in the big fashion houses.
- What do you do with your knives and forks after your picnic? This designer has made hers into an amazing hat and necklace.
- And can you believe that these dresses are made of toilet paper? These are the winners of a Toilet Paper Wedding Dress contest!
- Everyone needs shoes. Shoes made from old car tyres are easy and cheap to make and you never need new ones.

4 Read the article again. Match the photos 1–5 to pictures a–e.

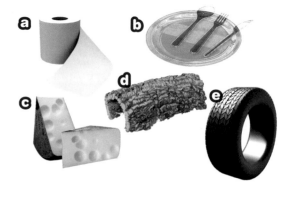

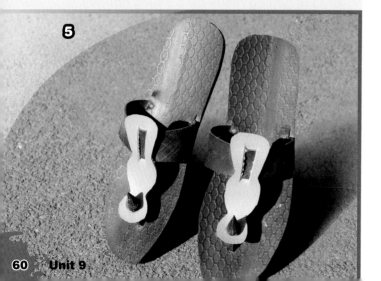

PRONUNCIATION   Words beginning with /s/, /ʃ/, /tʃ/

5 Look at the words and think about the first sound. Put the words into the right column.

> change   cheese   chilli   sea   shirt   shoes   shorts   sister   socks

/s/ sick	/ʃ/ shower	/tʃ/ chair

▶ 1.59 Listen and check. Then repeat.

6 ▶ 1.60 Now say this!

She sees six shoes and seven shirts in the cheese shop.

7 What other unusual things can we use to make clothes, shoes or jewellery?

LISTENING

8 ▶ 1.61 Listen to three people talking about their ideas for unusual things to use to make clothes or jewellery. Complete the table.

 Kris
 Sonya
 Felipe

	What is it?	What is it made of?
Kris		
Sonya		
Felipe		

9 ▶ 1.61 Listen again. Complete the sentence three times: once for Kris, once for Sonya and once for Felipe.

It's a really good idea to make clothes/jewellery out of .... because you've got .... when you ....

WRITING

10 Now think of your own idea for clothes or jewellery made of unusual materials. Make notes and give reasons for your choice.

11 Write a short paragraph about your idea.

Use the example sentence in Exercise 9 to help you.

My idea is to make .... out of .... because ...

Read your idea to the class.

10 Buying things
Are the sunglasses in the sale?

VOCABULARY AND LISTENING

1 Find these things in the pictures.

make-up   purse   shop assistant
shopping centre   sign   sunglasses   wallet

2 ▶1.62 Listen to Part 1 and answer the questions.

1 What does Jack want to buy today?
2 Why does he hope they are in the sale?

3 ▶1.63 Listen to Part 2 and answer the questions.

1 How much is the black wallet?
2 Why does Molly want to buy some make-up?

4 ▶1.62–1.63 Listen again to Parts 1 and 2. Choose the right word.

1 Jack went to *New York / the shopping centre* last week.
2 *Jack / Ravi* doesn't like spending money.
3 The black wallet in the sale is *half price / full price*.
4 Wallets are *cheaper / more expensive* in the shopping centre than in the market.
5 Molly *wants to / doesn't want to* buy a purse.
6 Ravi *wants some help / doesn't want any help* from the shop assistant.

5 Put the words from the box into the right column.

~~earring~~   ~~jewellery~~   leather   make-up
market   money   plastic   purse
sale   shop   wallet   wool

Countable nouns	Uncountable nouns
earring	jewellery

GRAMMAR *some, any, a bit of, a few, a lot of*

> There are some sales on today.
> Well, I want to spend some money today.
> There weren't any sales last week.
> You never want to spend any money!
> Look, there are a lot of purses and wallets.
> That's a lot of money.
> Molly wants to buy a bit of make-up.
> There are a few wallets over there.

→ Grammar reference **page 152**

6 Look at the sentences above from Jack, Molly and Ravi's conversation.

Now choose C (countable), U (uncountable) or C and U to complete the rules.

1 We use some in positive sentences with *C / U / C and U* nouns.

2 We use any in negative sentences with *C / U / C and U* nouns.

3 We use a lot of with *C / U / C and U* nouns.

4 We use a bit of with *C / U / C and U* nouns.

5 We use a few with *C / U / C and U* nouns.

7 Match the sentences to the pictures.

1 She's wearing a bit of jewellery.
2 He's got a few books.
3 She's wearing a lot of jewellery.
4 He's got a lot of books.

8 Look at the pictures. Complete the sentences with *a bit of, a few* or *a lot of.*

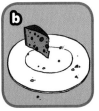

1 There are .... socks on the bed.
2 There's .... cake left.
3 We've got .... eggs in the fridge.
4 There are .... books on the shelf.
5 She's got .... money in her wallet.
6 I only ate .... breakfast this morning.

Corpus challenge

Which sentence is correct?
A Bring a ball and any water.
B I'm sorry, but I haven't got some milk.
C We had fun at the party and we played a lot of games.

PRONUNCIATION   Weak forms: /ə/

9 ▶1.64 Listen and repeat.

1 I want a bit of paper.
2 He took a few photos.
3 There were a lot of people.

10 Read the sentences from Exercise 8 aloud with your partner. Take turns.

About you

11 Make notes.
- Name a shopping centre or department store in your town.
- Do you like going there? Why? / Why not?
- Do you like shopping there? Why? / Why not?
- Has it got a sale at the moment?
- Are things usually cheaper there than in the other shops in your town?
- When you go to the shopping centre, what do you usually buy?

Now share your ideas with your partner.

Buying and selling online

1 Discuss these questions.

- What clothes websites do you know or like to visit?
- Do you like buying clothes online? Why? / Why not?

READING

2 Read the article about Matt Walls and answer the questions.

1 What is the name of Matt's company?
2 What does it sell?

3 Read the article again and answer the questions.

1 What kind of website did Matt and his friends start first?
2 What did they want people to do?
3 Why didn't this idea work?
4 What did they have a lot of fun doing?
5 When did they start Snorgtees?
6 How much do people get when Snorgtees choose their idea for a T-shirt?
7 Do you agree with Matt's advice?
8 Do you have any other advice?

SNORGTEES

HOME PRODUCTS ABOUT US CONTACT US SALE   VIEW BASKET

Matt Walls started the online company Snorgtees with a friend. This is how it began. Matt and a friend had the idea to start a funny website. They wanted people to add their own ideas and funny things. After that, they hoped to put some of the funniest ideas on T–shirts and sell them. The site didn't grow as fast as they hoped because people didn't add a lot of ideas. But Matt and his friend really enjoyed thinking of ideas for funny T-shirts, so they decided to start another website just for selling the T-shirts … and Snorgtees was born! That was in 2004.

People can send in their ideas for T-shirts to Matt and he and his team choose the best ones. They get $150 if the team decides to put their idea onto a T-shirt.

Here is Matt's advice for young entrepreneurs:

- Think carefully about what to sell online. It's important to make sure people want what you want to sell!

- Believe you can do it. Most people didn't think Snorgtees was a great idea in the beginning but Matt and his friends did – and they were right.

- Remember that starting a company is hard work. Some people think Matt and his friends sit around all day and talk about funny ideas. Actually, they spend most of the time working.

RECENTLY VIEWED ITEMS

4 Look again at the T-shirts from the Snorgtees site. Do you think they are funny? Work with a partner. Think of at least two funny T-shirts of your own. Show them to the class.

LISTENING

5 ▶1.65 **Listen and tick (✔) the correct picture.**

1 A  B

2 A  B

3 A  B

4 A  B

5 A  B

6 ▶1.65 **Listen again. Complete the sentences from the conversation. Use the words in the box.**

anyway	buy	come	doing	finally
long	more	problem	size	well

1 What are you .... here at the shopping centre?
2 Now I come to the shops to .... things.
3 Is there a .... with your computer?
4 It's a .... story.
5 Tell me ....!
6 .... , I found a great jacket on the internet.
7 After that, we waited and waited but it didn't ....
8 Then, six days later, it .... arrived.
9 But the jacket was the wrong ....
10 .... , guess what I bought today.

▶1.66 **Listen and check. Then repeat.**

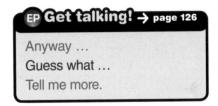

EP **Get talking!** → **page 126**

Anyway …
Guess what …
Tell me more.

7 Act out the story with your partner. Use the sentences from Exercise 6 and the pictures from Exercise 5 to help you.

WRITING

Prepare to write – A story

GET READY Read the story about the jacket on page 129. Find and underline these words in the story:
after that, *after (two weeks)*, *(six days) later*, *finally*

PLAN Imagine you tried to buy something online and there was a problem.
Read the questions and make notes.
1 What did you want to buy? Describe it and say why you liked it.
2 How did you buy it? Did you use a credit card? Whose card did you use?
3 How long did it take to come?
4 What happened when it arrived? What was wrong with it?
5 What did you do?
6 What was the end of the story?

WRITE Write your story in about 50 words. Try to link the events in your story with *after*, *after that*, *later* and *finally*. Start with these words:

I wanted to buy a .... , so I looked on the internet. I found one on this fantastic website and …

IMPROVE Read your own story and your partner's. Check for mistakes.
Give your partner two ideas to make their story better. Use your partner's advice and rewrite your story.

Culture
Hollywood

1 Look at the picture of the sign below.

   1 Which country is this sign in?

   2 What is 'Hollywood'?

   3 What is Hollywood famous for?

2 ▶2.02 Listen to a tour guide answering questions about Hollywood. In which month do the Oscars happen?

3 ▶2.02 Listen to the conversation again. Number the questions in the order you hear them.

When did the first film studio open?	☐
Do the Academy Awards still happen in Hollywood?	☐
What's the Walk of Fame?	☐
Is the town of Hollywood older than the sign?	☐
How old is the Hollywood sign?	1
When exactly was the Golden Age of Hollywood?	☐

4 ▶2.02 Work in groups of three. Listen again and then discuss your answers.

Student A: Listen to the answers for questions 1 and 4 and make notes.

Student B: Listen to the answers for questions 2 and 5 and make notes.

Student C: Listen to the answers for questions 3 and 6 and make notes.

5 Read about the Oscar statuette.

- The official name for the Oscar is the Academy Award of Merit.
- Emil Jannings won the first Academy Award for Best Actor in 1929.
- The Academy of Motion Pictures, Arts and Sciences first used the name Oscar in 1939.
- The awards are not only for actors. They also include Best Picture, Best Director, Best Costume Design, Best Song, Best Make-up and many others.
- The statuette is standing on a reel of film.
- The statuette is holding a sword.
- Each Oscar has a different number.
- It takes about four weeks to make 50 Oscars for the Academy Awards ceremony.
- Each Oscar is gold-plated.
- An Oscar is 35 centimetres high.
- An Oscar weighs almost four kilos.

6 Find the 'reel of film' and the 'sword' in the picture. Discuss your answers to the questions. What do you think?

1 Why is the statuette standing on a reel of film?
2 Why does each Oscar have a different number?
3 Why is the Oscar holding a sword?
4 Why is the statuette called 'Oscar'?
5 How many Oscars does the Academy give each year?
6 Hold something that weighs four kilos in your hand. Is an Oscar heavy or light?

You can find some answers on page 130.

Project — Make a poster

Work with a partner.
EITHER
Find out the names of the five Hollywood Film Studios of the Golden Age.
Choose *one* of the film studios. Answer the questions about it.
- What are the names of some of this studio's famous actors from this time?
- Did these actors win any Oscars?
- What are the names of some of this studio's famous films from this time?
- What Oscars did the film studio win for some of its films?
OR
Choose a film. Answer the questions about it.
- What are the names of some of the actors in the film?
- Which studio made the film?
- Did the film win any Oscars? Which ones?

Make a poster about your film studio or film.

11 Eating out
Which restaurant is better?

READING AND VOCABULARY

Pizza Palace

Come and have your
party here in our party room
– space for 30 guests!

Party menu

Pizzas
Margherita
Mushroom

Dessert
Ice cream – eat as much
as you want!

Drinks
Lemonade, cola

Price
£10.00 per person

Call us six months before your party to book –
we are very popular!

Birthday cake available

Easy Burgers

Fantastic party room – 30 guests

We play all your favourite music videos
while you eat!

Party menu

Main course
• Chicken legs
• Fresh vegetables
  or salad
• Burger
• Chips

Dessert
• Fruit salad and
  cream

Drinks
• Mineral water,
  lemonade

Price £13.00 per person

Our parties are very popular – book six months
before your birthday

Order our chef's amazing birthday cake

1 Read the restaurant advertisements. Find these things in the pictures.

> burgers   chicken legs   cola   ice cream   lemonade
> mineral water   mushroom   pizza   salad

▶ 2.03 Then listen and repeat.

2 Read the advertisements again. Are the sentences right (✔) or wrong (✗)?

1 The food at Easy Burgers looks healthier.
2 Pizza Palace is more expensive than Easy Burgers.
3 You can't get a birthday cake at either restaurant.
4 The menu at Easy Burgers is longer than the one at Pizza Palace.
5 You can watch something while you eat at Easy Burgers.
6 Easy Burgers and Pizza Palace are both popular.

GRAMMAR   *as ... as*

3 Read what Nicky thinks and complete the sentences with *the same* or *different*.

1 We use *as ... as* to say that two things are ....
2 We use *not as ... as* to say that two things are ....

→ Grammar reference **page 153**

> Pizza Palace is as popular as Easy Burgers.

> The birthday cake at Pizza Palace isn't as good as the one at Easy Burgers.

> Pizza Palace isn't as expensive as Easy Burgers.

Comparative adjectives

4 Write the comparatives of the adjectives and put them into the right column.

| beautiful | busy | cold | dirty | exciting | fat | funny |
| hot | large | late | long | new | popular | tall | thin |

short adjectives				long adjectives
add -er	*add -r*	*change to -ier*	*double the last letter and add -er*	*use 'more'*
short – shorter	nice – nicer	healthy – healthier	big – bigger	expensive – more expensive

→ Grammar reference **page 153**

5 Compare these pairs of things. Write two sentences for each pair using the adjectives given.

0 oranges ... lemons   *healthy / sweet*
   Lemons are as healthy as oranges. Oranges are sweeter than lemons.
1 trains ... buses   *comfortable / slow*
2 maths ... English   *easy / interesting*
3 cats ... dogs   *friendly / noisy*
4 your country ... the UK   *hot / big*
5 Ronaldo ... Messi   *young / famous*

> **Corpus challenge**
> **Can you correct this sentence?**
> The tickets for adults cost £25 but the tickets for students are more cheaper.

LISTENING

6 ▶2.04 Listen to Nicky. Which restaurant is she booking for her party?

7 Practise saying these prices, dates, times and numbers. Write some more to test your partner.

| £11.50 | £13.00 | April 8th | June 12th |
| 7.30 | 6.00 | 89 | 76 |

8 ▶2.04 Listen again and complete Nicky's notes.

Notes about my party!	
Date of party	(1)
Number of people	(2)
Price per person	(3) £
Time of party	(4)
Which number bus to get	(5)

> **EP Get talking!** → page 126
> Actually ...
> Sure, no problem.
> Of course.
> Oh no, that's too ...

WRITING AND SPEAKING

9 Write an advertisement for a party at a restaurant. Think of:
• size of party room   • drinks
• food   • price
Give your advertisement to your teacher.

10 Now work in pairs. Your teacher will give you two different advertisements. Compare the restaurants with your partner.
• Choose one of the restaurants for your party.
• Whose restaurant did you choose?
• Did anyone choose your restaurant?

STREET FOOD
around the world

In lots of countries around the world, street food is very popular. In Colombia, a favourite is *arepas*, a lovely kind of bread cake, often made with cheese. In India, you can get wonderful rice dishes with vegetables. These are often served with puri, made with flour and water or yogurt. On the streets of Thailand, you can buy fish soup, grilled chicken and lots of different kinds of noodles. For dessert, you can have fried bananas, fresh fruit pancakes or Thai sweets. In Germany, sausages are popular and in France, they serve lovely pancakes called crepes.

In many ways, street food is better than restaurant food. It's much cheaper and you know it's fresh because you watch the chef prepare and cook it in front of you. It's also a lot more fun to eat. People often buy and eat food outside at places like music festivals and also at sports events like football matches. At the seaside in many countries, people eat chips, ice cream and seafood.

READING AND VOCABULARY

1 Read the article about street food. What food is shown in each picture? Find the words in paragraph 1 of the article.

2 Answer the questions in groups.

   1 Would you like to eat any of the street food in the pictures?

   2 What kind of street food do you have in your country?

   3 Which is your favourite? How often do you eat it?

PRONUNCIATION /ʌ/ and /ɒ/

3 ▶ 2.06 Listen to the words and repeat them. Then put them in the right column.

c̶o̶f̶f̶e̶e̶ c̶u̶p̶ h<u>o</u>rrible l<u>o</u>vely much   m<u>u</u>shroom <u>o</u>melette <u>o</u>ne <u>o</u>nion   s<u>au</u>sage want what

/ʌ/	/ɒ/
cup	coffee

▶ 2.07 Listen and check your answers.

LISTENING

4 ▶ 2.08 You'll hear a girl at a street food festival. What does the girl order?

5 Complete the conversation from the recording.

Girl: Excuse me, what are you selling?

Seller: It's called paella. It's from **(1)** .... It's made with seafood, **(2)** .... , vegetables and **(3)** ....

Girl: Oh. What's it like?

Seller: It's **(4)** .... ! Would you like to try some?

Girl: Yes, please. How **(5)** .... is it?

Seller: It's $4.50 for a small plate or **(6)** $............................ for a large plate.

Girl: I'll have a small plate, please.

Seller: That's **(7)** $............................ , please.

Girl: Here you **(8)** ....

Seller: Thanks. I hope you **(9)** .... it!

▶ 2.08 **Listen again and check. Then practise the conversation with a partner.**

SPEAKING

6 Imagine you are at the street-food festival. Ask about and order the food in the pictures.

Empanadas
75 cents each
Made with meat, onions, chilli and tomatoes

Argentina

Yaki soba
Fried noodles with cabbage, carrot, meat and onions
small bowl $4.50
large bowl $7.00

Japan

Shish kebab
Grilled chicken or lamb
$1.50 each

Turkey

Tacos
Tortilla with meat
$5.00

Mexico

12 The latest technology
Supercomputers

READING AND VOCABULARY

1 Look at the pictures and read the magazine article. Match each paragraph to a picture.

2 Find a word in the article for each definition.

1 This describes cameras, computers and clocks that record information as 0s or 1s.
d _ _ _ _ _ _

2 This has moving parts and helps humans to do work.
m _ _ _ _ _ _

3 This is how much information a computer can hold.
m _ _ _ _ _

4 This is a dangerous computer program.
v _ _ _ _

5 You can see these in the sky at night.
s _ _ _ _

6 This means to copy information onto your computer.
d _ _ _ _ _ _ _

3 Read the article again. Then cover it and just look at the pictures. Work with a partner. Can you remember what the article said about each thing? Make notes. Compare your notes with the article.

Computers and the modern world

☐ The first 'computers' were simple counting machines such as the abacus. Digital computers only arrived in the 1940s. These were much faster than the earlier counting machines but they needed a lot of space. One of the most famous was called Colossus and it was the size of a large living room.

☐ Today, the smallest mobile phones have more memory than the biggest of those early computers. In fact, every year, computers get smaller, faster and cheaper. But there are still some very large computers in the world. These are called supercomputers. One of the biggest and fastest is the Hopper computer. It has a picture of the American computer scientist Grace Hopper on it. Scientists use it to study the weather and the physics of the stars.

☐ Different supercomputers are good at different things. Watson is the best at answering quiz questions. It's very difficult for computers to do this well, because they need to understand human language. Watson is still worse than humans at doing this but it's better than any other computer.

☐ Modern computers are wonderful but they are not perfect. One of the worst problems is computer viruses. You can lose a lot of information if one of these gets into your machine. The most important thing to remember is to be very careful about what you download onto your computer.

GRAMMAR Superlative adjectives

4 Look at the examples of superlatives. Read the article again and find all the superlatives.

the smallest mobile phone you can buy
the most important thing to remember

5 Complete the tables.

Regular

Adjective	Comparative	Superlative
big	bigger	the biggest
famous	more famous	the most famous
early		
thin		
heavy		
beautiful		
young		
popular		

Irregular

Adjective	Comparative	Superlative
good		
bad		

→ Grammar reference **page 154**

ⓒ Corpus challenge

Can you correct this sentence?
I like it so much because it is the famous game in the world.

PRONUNCIATION Stress in superlatives

6 ▶2.09 Listen and repeat the words. Put them into the right column of the table.

the biggest   the cleverest
the quickest   the most exciting
the most expensive   the friendliest
the nicest   the worst

oO	oOo	oOoo	oooOo
	the biggest		

▶2.10 Listen and check.

SPEAKING

7 Look at the three mobile phones. Compare them with a partner. Use some of these adjectives:

cheap/expensive   big/small
thick/thin   heavy/light   good/bad
easy/difficult to use

The battery on the Storm is better than the battery on the Bluebird.
The battery on the Bluebird is the worst.
The battery on the Cloud 7 is the best.

	Storm	Bluebird	Cloud 7
Price	£299	£355	£450
Size	115 x 58 x 9 mm	116 x 61 x 12 mm	135 x 67 x 17 mm
Weight	130 g	142 g	155 g
Camera	★★★☆☆	★★☆☆☆	★★★★☆
Battery	★★☆☆☆	★☆☆☆☆	★★★☆☆
Easy to use?	★★★★☆	★★★☆☆	★★★★☆

About you

8 Write true sentences with superlatives. Use the ideas below or your own ideas.
The most famous person in my country is the Queen.

Compare your answers with a partner.

boring   noisy
easy   old
famous   popular
good

school subject
person in my family
person in my country
computer game I play
show on TV
place in my country
thing I have

Me and my computer

VOCABULARY

1 Label the picture with the words in the box.

> keyboard   laptop   mouse   tablet   printer   screen   speaker

▶ 2.11 **Listen and check. Then repeat the words.**

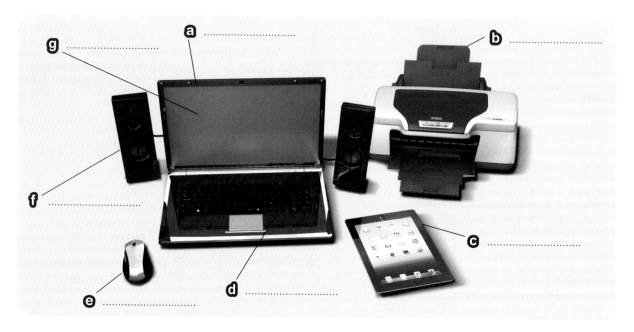

a ....
b ....
c ....
d ....
e ....
f ....
g ....

2 Complete each phrase with one or more of the words.

> clothes   films   friends
> games   homework
> the internet   music or pictures
> videos   websites

People go online to …
- use ....
- chat to ....
- download ....
- watch ....
- play ....
- do ....
- visit ....
- buy ....

3 Write six sentences about how often you do the things in Exercise 2. Use these words.

> sometimes   often   never
> once a week/month
> every day/afternoon/evening

I play games online once a week.

SPEAKING

4 Read the survey. Choose three or four questions. Walk around the class asking your questions.

Computer survey

How many hours a day do you spend online?

What's your favourite website?

Do you play computer games? If yes, which ones?

How often do you chat to your friends online?

How often do you shop online? What do you buy?

5 Write some sentences about what you found out.

The most popular computer game in our class is …
Zara doesn't play as many computer games as Deniz.

3 Look at the example. Then answer the questions. You can use a calculator.

$c = \pi d$	$a = \pi r^2$
$c = 3.14 \times d$	$a = \pi \times 11^2$
$c = 3.14 \times 22$	$a = \pi \times 121$
$c = 69.08$ cm	$a = 3.14 \times 121$
	$a = 379.94$ cm^2

11cm

22cm

1 A circle has a diameter of 10 cm. What is its circumference?
2 A circle has a radius of 8 cm. What is its diameter?
3 A circle has a diameter of 26 cm. What is its radius?
4 A circle has a radius of 10 cm. What is its area?
5 A circle has a diameter of 18 cm What is its area?

4 With a partner, write five similar questions and give them to another pair to do.

5 Now answer these questions.

1 A bicycle wheel has a radius of 31.85 cm. How far will the bicycle go if the wheel turns once?
2 Which circle has the bigger radius?
  Circle A: diameter 15.5 cm
  Circle B: circumference 40 cm
3 A farmer wants to make a pool for his ducks with circumference of 45 m. What is the area of the pool?
4 The radius of the Earth is 6,371 km. What is its circumference?

Project Calculate pi

For this activity, you will need:
• a circular object, e.g. a lid, DVD, coin, plate
• a piece of string
• a ruler
• a calculator

1 Measure the diameter of the object with the ruler.
2 Measure the circumference of the object using the piece of string.
3 Divide the circumference by the diameter.
4 Make a table on the board showing each pair's results.

Whose number is the closest to pi? How big was their object? What does this tell you about measuring pi?

Review 3
Units 9–12

VOCABULARY

1 **Complete the sentences with the words in the box.**

> ~~digital~~   download   half price   keyboard
> pocket   sign   size   tablets   wallet

0 I really like that new ......<u>digital</u>...... camera.

1 This computer was £500 last week. Now it's £250. That's ....

2 Look. There's a .... over there on the wall. It says 'Restaurant this way'.

3 My dad gave me a .... for my birthday. And he put £20 in it!

4 I want to buy a new coat. I like that one but it's only got one ....

5 These shoes are the wrong .... They're much too big.

6 The .... on that new computer is very small. It's difficult to see the letters.

7 Most people .... music from the internet these days. They don't buy CDs or records.

8 At my new school, all the students have .... They don't have books.

2 **Put the words into the right group.**

> ~~cap~~   ~~cola~~   jacket   jewellery   jumper
> lemonade   mineral water   mushroom
> omelette   onion   sausage   shorts
> socks   swimming costume

Things you can eat and drink	Things you can wear
cola	cap

3 **Write the words.**

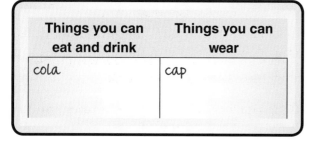

GRAMMAR

4 ⊙ **Choose the right word to complete the sentences.**

1 I bought a new T-shirt because *my / mine* is old.

2 Do you have *any / a* present for me?

3 I love my room because it's *bigger / biggest* than my old room.

4 You can find different bands and the *better / best* music.

⊙ **Correct the mistakes in these sentences.**

5 You can wear yours sports clothes.

6 I bought a new jeans and a shirt.

7 I bought them because they were very cheaper: they cost only £5 each!

8 It was the great holiday ever.

5 **Complete the sentences with *a bit of* or *a few*.**

0 Would you like ...<u>a bit of</u>... chocolate?

1 Can I have .... paper, please?

2 We saw .... people on the train today.

3 There are .... advertisements in the newspaper.

4 I'm hungry! Can I have .... cake?

5 .... companies have only online shopping.

6 I'd like .... cheese in my sandwich, please.

7 She had .... make-up on her T-shirt.

8 He was sick in bed for .... days.

6 Complete the sentences with the comparative or superlative form of the adjective in brackets.

0 Oranges are .... _sweeter than_ .... lemons. (sweet)

00 All these books are old but this one is .... _the oldest_ .... (old)

1 You are always .... me! (busy)

2 All the students' work is good today but yours is .... (good)

3 Football is .... sport in the UK. (popular)

4 I liked your story. It was .... mine. (funny)

5 Our cat is .... it was two years ago. (thin)

6 That café has .... hot chocolate in town. (bad)

7 The chairs in this classroom are .... (comfortable) in the school.

8 The new phones are .... the old ones. (clever)

READING

7 Read the text and answer the question.

Tim has got three sisters – Beth, Mary and Alice. Beth is three years younger than Tim and seven years younger than Mary. Alice is the youngest. She's six years old. She's one year younger than Beth.

How old are Tim, Beth and Mary?

LISTENING

8 ▶2.14 Listen and choose the right answer.

0 How many people were at the party?

A **5**   B **15**   Ⓒ **50**

1 What does the man want to buy?

A   B   C

2 Where does the woman come from?

A **England**   B **Scotland**   C **Wales**

3 What time is the next train?

A   B   C

4 What is in the sale this week?

A   B   C

5 How much is the menu per person?

A **£8**   B **£11**   C **£14**

SPEAKING

9 Put the words in the right order to make questions.

1 favourite / what / are / clothes / your / ?

2 like / you / shopping / going / do / ?

3 can / cook / you / what / ?

4 like / newest / you / do / the / smartphones / ?

Ask and answer the questions with your partner. Take turns to speak.

10 Now talk about some of your favourite things. Take turns to speak.

Tell me about some of your favourite things.

I've got a favourite pair of jeans. I like them very much because …

13 Healthy bodies
What's the matter?

VOCABULARY

1 Match each sentence to a picture.

1 I've got a cold.
2 I hurt my leg.
3 I've got a broken arm. *a*
4 My eye hurts.
5 I feel sick.
6 I've got a stomach ache.
7 I've got a temperature.
8 I've got toothache.
9 I've got a pain in my foot.
10 I've got a headache.

▶ 2.15 Listen and check. Then repeat.

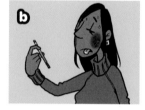
a

b

c

d

e

f

g

h

i

j

LISTENING

2 ▶ 2.16 You'll hear three conversations. Choose the right health problem for each person.

Health problem

	A	B
1		
2		
3		

3 ▶ 2.16 Listen again. Match the advice with the health problems. Write 1, 2 or 3.

don't do any sports ☐
eat fruit and vegetables ☐
don't go to bed late ☐
go to hospital ☐ 1
don't walk ☐
rest ☐
go to bed now ☐
drink a lot ☐

About you

4 Talk to your partner. Tell your partner about your last health problem.
 • describe the problem
 I had a headache and a stomach ache.
 • say when it happened
 It started on Friday.
 • explain what you did
 I took some medicine and went to bed.

GRAMMAR *should/shouldn't*

5 Look at these examples from the recording. Then choose the right word to complete sentences 1–3.

You should go to bed.
You shouldn't walk on that leg.

> **1** We use *should* when we think something is a *good / bad* idea.
> **2** We use *shouldn't* when we think something is a *good / bad* idea.
> **3** The verb after *should* is *always / never* the infinitive without 'to'.

→ Grammar reference **page 155**

6 Look at these examples from the recording. Match the questions to the answers. Notice how we make questions with *should*.

I should ——————→ Should I

1 *Should I stop doing sports?*
2 *Should I take some medicine?*
3 *When should I drink it?*

a *No, you shouldn't.*
b *Every evening before bed.*
c *Yes, you should.*

▶ 2.17 Listen and check. Then repeat.

7 Read the problems (1–8) and choose the best advice for each one (a–h). Then complete the advice with *should/shouldn't*. There may be more than one possible answer.

1 My hand hurts a bit today.
2 I've got a pain in my foot.
3 I've got a headache and a temperature.
4 I feel a bit sick.
5 My eyes hurt.
6 I can't move my leg at all. I think it's broken.
7 I feel very tired.
8 I've got a bad cold.

a You .... go to bed earlier.
b You .... take some medicine and go to bed.
c You .... play tennis.
d You .... go to school.
e You .... wear more comfortable shoes.
f You .... go to hospital.
g You .... eat anything.
h You .... stop watching TV.

> ⊙ **Corpus challenge**
>
> **Can you correct this sentence?**
> I think you should to bring a scarf.

SPEAKING

8 Read the example conversation on the right. Have similar conversations with your partner. Choose a different question from the box each time. Use health problems and advice from this lesson, or use your own ideas.

> **Asking about health problems**
> What's the matter?
> What's wrong?
> Are you OK?

PRONUNCIATION Silent consonants

9 Some words in English have silent consonants. Find one silent consonant in each word.

> shou(l)d   answer   would   wrong   half
> Wednesday   listen   talk   walk   knife

▶ 2.18 Listen and check. Then repeat.

What's the matter?

I've got a temperature. What should I do?

You should rest. You should drink lots of water. You shouldn't go to school.

▶ Video extra Healthy bodies **81**

You should enter the race!

Six weeks later...

LISTENING AND VOCABULARY

1 Look at the pictures and the words. Can you guess what is happening in the story?

> advice   eat well   enter a race   finish a race   five kilometres   get fit

2 ▶2.19 Look at the pictures and listen. Are the sentences right (✔) or wrong (✘)?

1 Jack sees a notice about a five-kilometre race.
2 Ravi and Molly can do the race with Jack.
3 Jack wants to do the race with Ravi and Molly.
4 Jack is worried about the price of sports clothes and trainers.
5 Jack is happy to get up early.
6 Jack can go cycling as well as running.
7 Jack is pleased to see Molly and Ravi at the race.

3 ▶2.19 Listen again. Write R (Ravi) and/or M (Molly) in the second column of the table.

Advice for Jack	Who gave him this advice?	What do you think? Good or bad advice? Say why!
1 You should buy special running clothes.		
2 You should get some good trainers.		
3 You should go running every day.		
4 You should go to bed early every night.		
5 You shouldn't watch TV or play on the computer.		
6 You should eat well and drink lots of water.		
7 You shouldn't have any chocolate or cake.		
8 As well as running, you should go swimming or cycling.		
9 You should do exercises to make your legs stronger.		

4 Work with a partner. Complete the third column of the table. Put a G for good advice and a B for bad advice.

READING

5 Read the magazine article. Match the headings to the paragraphs.

A Getting started   **C** Running is good for you

B Enter a race!   **D** Make each day different

Yes, you can run 5 km in six weeks!

1 ....

Every day in newspapers and magazines there are articles telling us we should exercise more. And scientists now say that running is one of the best ways to keep fit. It can make you feel better and look better. Some say it can even make you live longer.

2 ....

All you need for running are some comfortable clothes and a pair of trainers. You don't need to buy special clothes but you should get a good pair of trainers. And remember – you should always buy trainers for running one size larger than your usual shoes.

3 ....

Some people find running boring, so go cycling or swimming instead sometimes. Also, you shouldn't exercise every day. It's very important to rest two or three times a week. You should eat well and drink lots of water but you can still have nice things like chocolate sometimes. Do some leg and stomach exercises every week as well, because this makes you stronger and helps you run better.

4 ....

If you're a beginner, there are lots of ways to make exercise fun. You can join a club or you can exercise with a friend. Another idea is to enter a race. This can give you a reason to train and keep you interested in running.

6 Find the advice in the article. Compare it with Molly and Ravi's advice. Is it the same?

WRITING

7 Look at these questions on an internet chat page. The people are all asking for advice.

EP Get talking! → page 127

That's a shame.
Oh dear.
Never mind.

 My family and I are going on a cycling holiday soon but I'm not very fit. Can you give me some advice?

comment

 I'm starting at a new school soon and I don't know anyone. How can I make friends?

comment

 I want to improve my English. It's really bad! What should I do?

comment

Work with a partner. Choose a problem. Together, think of three pieces of advice for the person.

8 Give a short answer to the problem. Write about 25 words.

It's important to …   You should/shouldn't …   Another idea is to …

9 Compare your paragraph with other students' paragraphs. Who gave the best advice?

14 In the town
Turn right at the roundabout

This is my town. It's small but very pretty. A river goes through the town centre and there are three bridges going across it. Between the road and the river, there's a market. Next to the market is a really nice café. There are also some shops in the town. Opposite the shops, there's a bank, a museum and a restaurant. The restaurant is near the train station, and beside the train station there's a post office. There's also a supermarket on that street. In front of the supermarket, there's a car park. We have a hospital too but that's outside the town.

VOCABULARY

1 Read the description of the town and look at the map. Find these things on the map.

> a bridge   buildings
> a park   a river
> a roundabout   streets
> traffic lights

2 Find a place where you can:

0 see a film   *cinema*
1 send a letter
2 stay the night
3 buy food
4 borrow a book
5 study
6 eat a meal
7 get some money
8 buy petrol
9 find a police officer
10 get better
11 go swimming
12 catch a bus

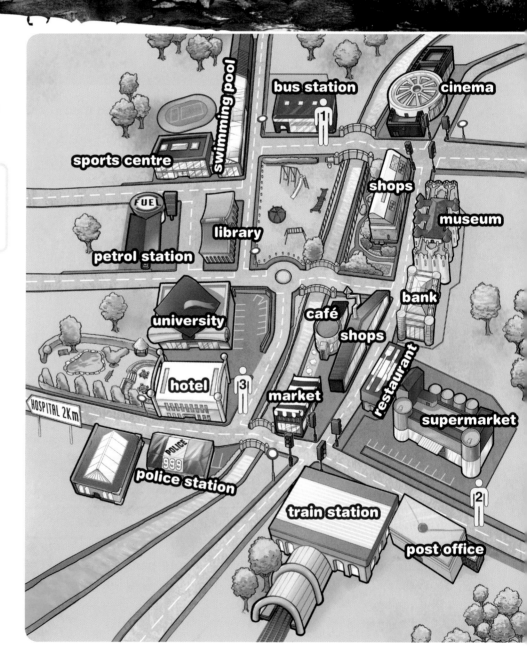

GRAMMAR Prepositions

3 Read the description of the town and look at the map.
Complete each sentence with a different preposition
from the text.

1 The river goes .... the town.
2 Hotel guests need to go .... the river to go
   to the market.
3 The hospital is .... the town.
4 There's a bus stop .... the sports centre.
5 There's a car park .... the supermarket.
6 The bank is .... the museum.
7 The hotel is .... the university.
8 There are some shops .... the museum.

→ Grammar reference **page 156**

→ Grammar reference **page 156**

> **◎Corpus challenge**
>
> **Can you correct this sentence?**
> **Choose the right preposition.**
> To get to my house, go ~~through~~
> Beat Street, turn right and it's
> the first house on the left.
> **A** opposite
> **B** along
> **C** beside

LISTENING

4 ▶2.21 **Find the people on the map.** **Each person wants to go somewhere.**
Listen to the conversations. Where does each person want to go?

Person 1 ....   Person 2 ....   Person 3 ....

SPEAKING Give directions

5 **Look at the directions. Match each sentence to a picture.**

1 Go past the train station.
2 Turn right at the traffic lights.
3 Go straight on.
4 The bank is on your right.
5 Drive along this road.
6 Turn left at the roundabout.

a

b

c

d

e

f

▶2.22 **Listen and check. Then repeat.**

6 **Make some conversations with your partner.
Decide where you are on the map and where
you want to go.**

Begin like this:

> *Excuse me. Is there a supermarket near here?*

> *Which way is the museum?*

WRITING

7 Write some directions to places from your
school. Give the directions to your teacher.

8 Listen to the directions. Can you say where
you are?

*Go out of the school and turn left. Take the
first road on the right. Walk past Café Brava.
Where are you?*

A trip to Edinburgh

READING

1 Look at the map and read the article about Edinburgh. Match places a–e on the map with these names.

> Edinburgh Castle
> Palace of Holyroodhouse
> Scottish Parliament
> St Giles' Cathedral
> Tourist Information Office

▶ 2.23 **Listen and check. Then repeat the names.**

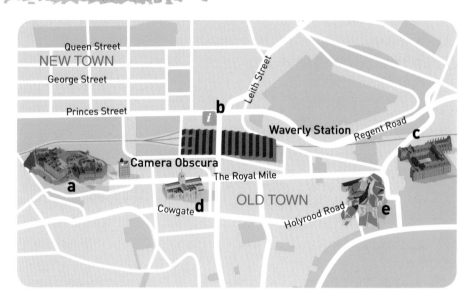

Visit Edinburgh!

Edinburgh isn't the biggest city in Scotland but it's very beautiful and has an amazing history. The best place to start your visit is Edinburgh Castle. This sits up on top of an old volcano and from here you can see the whole city below you. It gets very busy in the summer, so go as early as you can.

After visiting the castle, walk down the Royal Mile, through Edinburgh's 12th-century Old Town. Don't miss the Camera Obscura museum and St Giles' Cathedral. At the bottom of the Royal Mile is the Queen's Edinburgh home, the Palace of Holyroodhouse. When the Queen isn't there, you can visit the lovely rooms and gardens. Next to the Palace is the Scottish Parliament. This unusual building cost £415 million to build, and is a very interesting place to visit.

You should also go to Edinburgh's New Town to see the beautiful streets and enjoy its shops and cafés. The area isn't very new actually – it's over 200 years old! If you like shopping, you should go to Princes Street. This is where you can find Edinburgh's best shops.

If you haven't got much time, there are lots of different guided tours you can do – bus tours, walking tours, cycle tours and even ghost tours of the Old Town at night. You can get tickets for all of these at the Tourist Information Centre at no. 3 Princes Street.

2 Read the article again. Are sentences 1–7 right (A) or wrong (B)? If there isn't enough information to answer right or wrong, choose C (doesn't say).

0 Edinburgh is the largest city in Scotland.	A	(B)	C	
00 Edinburgh Castle is the oldest building in Edinburgh.	A	B	(C)	
1 Lots of people visit the castle in the summer.	A	B	C	
2 The castle opens at 8 am.	A	B	C	
3 It takes an hour to walk from Edinburgh Castle to Holyroodhouse.	A	B	C	
4 The Queen sometimes stays at Holyroodhouse.	A	B	C	
5 The Scottish Parliament building is closed to visitors.	A	B	C	
6 The shops in Edinburgh's New Town are expensive.	A	B	C	
7 All of Edinburgh's guided tours are on foot.	A	B	C	

LISTENING

3 ▶2.24 Listen to Rob talking to a friend about a visit to Edinburgh. Which place did Rob visit at each time?

Times
0 Friday evening
1 Saturday morning
2 Saturday afternoon
3 Sunday morning
4 Sunday afternoon

Places
A Cathedral
B Edinburgh Castle
C Holyroodhouse Palace
D Museum
E New Town
F Old Town
G Scottish Parliament

About you

4 Answer these questions for you. Then compare with a partner.
- Would you like to go to Edinburgh?
- What would you like to do there?
- Do you enjoy visiting cities?
- What kind of museums do you like best?

VOCABULARY

In English, it's possible to make new words by putting two words together: *bus + stop = bus stop*. Do you do this in your language too?

5 Match the words on the left to the words on the right to make new words.

cycle
police
walking
town   tour
bus   station
post   office
petrol   centre
train
sports

▶2.25 Listen and check.

PRONUNCIATION   Two-word nouns

6 ▶2.25 Listen again to the words in Exercise 5 and underline the stressed word.

cycle tour

In two-word nouns, which word does the stress usually fall on? Which one is different here? Listen again and repeat the words.

WRITING

Prepare to write — A city guide

GET READY Look at the article about Edinburgh again and find all the examples of *this* and *these*.

Complete the sentences about places in London with *this* or *these*.
1 Buckingham Palace is one of the Queen's homes. .... building has 775 rooms.
2 Oxford Street has many shops. .... are open until 7 pm most evenings.
3 There are lots of museums in London. Some of .... are free.
4 Hyde Park is in central London. .... is a great place for a picnic.

PLAN Make a list of interesting and famous places in your capital city. Choose three and make notes about them. Think about:
- where they are
- what you can do there
- why they are interesting

WRITE Write 50–60 words about your capital city. Use *this/these* in your paragraph.

CHECK Compare your paragraph with your partner's. Did you write about the same places? Correct any mistakes with *this/these*. Rewrite your paragraph.

Culture
Famous British people

1 Work with a partner. Look at the pictures of some people who are important to British culture. What do you know about them?

- Name?
- Date of birth? / Which century did he/she live in?
- Why is he/she important?

William Shakespeare

William Shakespeare was born on April 23rd 1564 and is one of the greatest writers in the history of the world. He wrote 37 plays and over 150 poems. He was very creative – when he did not have the right word, he invented a new one. We still use many of these words today.

John Lennon and Paul McCartney

John Lennon and Paul McCartney were born in Liverpool in the early 1940s. They started a band called The Beatles. During the 1960s, The Beatles were the most famous band in the world. Their music was new and exciting, and songs like *Hey Jude*, *Nowhere Man* and *Love Me Do* changed pop music forever.

Sir Isaac Newton

Isaac Newton was born on December 25th 1643. As a young man, he studied at Cambridge University. In 1687, he wrote one of the most important books in the history of science. It explained how gravity works, and how objects move. He also studied light and invented a new kind of telescope.

Richard Branson

Richard Branson was born in London in 1950. He did not do well at school. When he left, he started a magazine called *Student* and then he moved into the music business. Now he owns an airline, a train company and a mobile phone company. Richard Branson loves adventure and he tried four times to be the first person to fly round the world in a hot-air balloon. Now his company Virgin Galactic is planning to take people into space.

Queen Elizabeth I

Queen Elizabeth I was born in 1533. She was queen from 1558 to 1603 and never married. This was an exciting part of English history. There were new ideas about art and literature, more business, and more travel to new lands. It was the time when England first became an important country in the world.

GREAT
BRITONS

2 Read the text once and check your answers to Exercise 1.

3 Read the text again and answer the questions.

   1 How many plays did Shakespeare write?
   2 How did Shakespeare change the English language?
   3 Where were Lennon and McCartney born?
   4 When did The Beatles become very famous?
   5 Where did Isaac Newton go to university?
   6 What did Newton's book explain?
   7 What businesses does Richard Branson own now?
   8 What does Branson like doing in his free time?
   9 When did Queen Elizabeth I die?
  10 What changes happened when Elizabeth I was queen?

4 Read these quotations by the people on the opposite page.

   1 Life is what happens when you are busy making other plans.

   2 We build too many walls and not enough bridges.

   3 Better three hours too soon than a minute too late.

   4 You don't learn to walk by following rules. You learn by doing it and falling over.

   5 I have the heart of a man, not a woman. And I am not afraid of anything.

   6 Love is all you need.

   7 A fool[1] thinks himself wise[2] but a wise man knows he is a fool.

   8 If I have seen further than others, it is by standing on the shoulders of giants[3].

> [1] *fool – stupid person*
> [2] *wise – clever/intelligent*
> [3] *giant – very tall person*

5 Discuss the quotations in groups. What do they mean? Which are your favourites? Can you guess who said each one?

6 Put the sentences in order to make a mini biography of the scientist Stephen Hawking.

- While he was there, he became ill with motor neurone disease.
- He is often on TV, and was once in the TV show *The Simpsons*.
- He soon became an expert on black holes, gravity and the universe.
- Stephen Hawking was born in 1942 and studied physics at Cambridge University.
- This did not stop him from studying and working.
- He is very good at writing books which explain these subjects to ordinary people.

Project **Write a biography**

Find out about a person who is very important in your country.
- When were they born?
- Where are they from?
- Why are they famous?
- What did they do?

Write a mini biography about the person. Add a photograph and one or two quotes. Present your work to the class.

15 Weather and places
It was snowing yesterday at 5 pm

VOCABULARY

1 What's the weather like?
Match the sentences to
the pictures.

1	It's wet.	5	There's a thunderstorm.
2	It's sunny.	6	It's very windy.
3	It's foggy.	7	It's cloudy.
4	It's dry.	8	It's snowy.

▶ 2.26 Listen and check. Then repeat.

2 Ask and answer with a partner.

> What's the weather like in picture e?

> It's snowy.

3 Complete the table.

Noun	Adjective
cloud	cloudy
snow	
fog	
wind	
sun	
rain	

4 Choose the right word.

1 Look! It's very *snow / snowy* outside!
2 It's often *fog / foggy* in the autumn.
3 When it's very *wind / windy*, I like to fly my kite.
4 You shouldn't sit in the *sun / sunny* for a long time.
5 I don't like playing football in the *rain / rainy*.

LISTENING

5 ▶ 2.27 Jack, Ravi and Molly are finishing their weather project. At 2 pm yesterday, they talked to students in three different places around the world. Listen and write the names of the countries.

	Country	Time	Weather	What doing?
Anna				sleeping
Sanjiv				
Jens/ Eva				

6 ▶ 2.27 Listen again. Complete the *Time, Weather* and *What doing?* columns in the table.

7 What's the weather like in your town today? What's the temperature?

It isn't sunny. It's cloudy and it's very cold. The temperature is about 8 degrees.

GRAMMAR Past continuous

8 Complete 1 and 2 using the information from Exercise 6.

Anna Sanjiv Jens and Eva	was wasn't were weren't	sleeping 1 .... 2	at 2 pm UK time yesterday.

Questions				Short answers		
Were Was	he she you they	sleeping at 2 pm UK time yesterday?		Yes, No,	he she you they	was. wasn't. were. weren't.

→ Grammar reference **page 157**

9 Use the table above to make sentences and questions.

Anna wasn't eating dinner at 2 pm UK time yesterday. She ....
Jens and Eva weren't eating dinner at 2 pm UK time yesterday. They ....
Was Sanjiv eating dinner at 2 pm yesterday? Yes, ...

10 What was happening yesterday afternoon? Complete the sentences with the verb in the past continuous.

0 '...Was... Suzie ...helping... (help) her teacher?' 'Yes, ...she was...'

1 The boys .... (play) football in the park. They .... (not run) very fast because the grass was wet.

2 '................. you .... (climb) that tree?' 'No, I ....'

3 My friend .... (watch) TV. She .... (not tidy) her room.

4 '................. the students .... (working) on the computer?' 'Yes, ... '

5 '................. he .... (travel) alone?' 'No, ... '

Corpus challenge

Can you correct this sentence?
It ~~rains~~ in Taipei when we got there.

PRONUNCIATION *was, wasn't, were, weren't*

11 ▶2.28 **Listen and repeat.**

My brother was riding his bike.
My dad wasn't working in the garden.
Was it raining this morning?
The students were listening to the teacher.
The boys weren't playing computer games.
Were they talking?

SPEAKING

12 Ask and answer with your partner.

What were you doing …
… last Sunday afternoon at three o'clock?
… yesterday at seven o'clock?
… last Saturday at one o'clock?
… last Monday evening at six o'clock?
What was the weather like?

What were you doing last Sunday afternoon at three o'clock?

I was shopping with my mum. It was raining.

EP Get talking! → **page 127**

Just a minute.
Right.
So …

Strange stories

READING

1 Match the words in the box to the pictures.

What do you think each of these strange stories is about?

field   footprint   forest   lake   mountains   sky   snow   water

Are they real?

2 Read the two stories quickly. Check your answers to Exercise 1.

The Fens is a wet area in the east of England. There are large fields, farms and small villages. It's not the kind of place you usually find a wild tiger! In 1994, William Rooker thought he saw a large cat. It was larger than a normal cat and he thought it looked like a tiger. It was walking across a field, so he quickly took out his camera and filmed it. He wasn't the first person to see it but he was the first to film it. People called the animal the Fen Tiger.

Other people say they saw the Fen Tiger. Joan Peacock found the footprint in the photo in her garden. 'My dog was barking in the night,' she said, 'and in the morning I found these footprints.'

Many people in the Fens believe there is a Fen Tiger. Do you? Is it possible that there's a tiger living wild in England?

In 1951, a British explorer, Eric Shipton, was climbing in the high mountains of the Himalayas, south of Mount Everest. There were several climbers and Sherpas with him. As they were walking through the snow, they saw a line of footprints. They followed the footprints for 500 metres. The footprints were 33 cm long, 20 cm wide and a few centimetres deep. They were much too big to be a bear's. The Sherpas said they knew the animal. They said it usually lived in the forests and didn't often come up into the snow. Their name for the animal was the Yeti, or the Wild Man of the Snows.

Eric Shipton's photos of the footprints became famous around the world.

People still come back from the Himalayas today with stories of seeing the Yeti. One person found some of its black hair!

3 Read the stories again. Are the sentences right (✔) or wrong (✗)? Correct the wrong sentences.

1 The Fens is the name of a city in England.
2 William Rooker was the first person to see the Fen Tiger.
3 Joan Peacock saw the Fen Tiger in her garden.
4 Eric Shipton was climbing in a group.
5 The footprints were smaller than a bear's.
6 Yetis live most of the time in the forests.

4 Talk with a partner. What do you think?

- Is it possible for a tiger to live wild in England?
- If it isn't a tiger, what animal do you think it is?
- Is the Fen Tiger real, or is it just a story?
- Is the Yeti a man-ape from thousands of years ago?
- Are there many Yetis living in the forests around the Himalayas?
- Is the Yeti real, or is it just a story?

VOCABULARY

5 Give the names of …

1 two mountains
2 four animals that live in the mountains
3 two big areas of water in or near your country
4 four animals that live in or near water
5 two large areas of forest in or near your country
6 four animals that usually live in forests

6 Look at the pictures and complete the sentences with *long, wide, high, deep.*

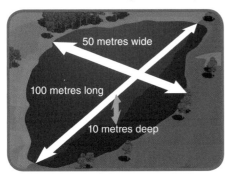

50 metres wide
100 metres long
10 metres deep

1000 metres high

1 Mount Everest is 8,848 metres ....
2 The Amazon River is 11 kilometres ....
  and 6,400 kilometres ....
3 Lake Titicaca is 107 metres ....

7 Work with a partner. Write a quiz.

The Mississippi River is
A 2,800 kilometres long.
B 3,800 kilometres long.
C 4,800 kilometres long.

LISTENING

8 ▶2.31 Peter was on holiday with a friend in Scotland last summer. They were looking for the Loch Ness Monster. Listen and answer the questions.

1 What was Peter's friend's name?
2 What was the weather like?

9 ▶2.31 Listen again and answer the questions.

1 What day of the week was it?
2 Did Peter wake up after or before his friend?
3 What could Peter see on the other side of the loch?
4 What did Peter think he could see in the water?
5 Why did Peter wait before he took the photo?
6 What did his friend see in the water?

WRITING

10 What other stories about strange animals do you know?

Work with a partner. Use the internet or reference books to find out more. Make notes and copy photos and pictures.

11 Work with your partner. Write a short article for *Strange Stories* magazine about when and where someone saw the strange animal.

Use the texts in Exercise 2 to help you.
Stick your article on paper with one or two of your pictures. Put it up in the classroom and talk about it to other students.

16 Amazing animals
He was looking at the gorillas ...

READING

1 Discuss the questions with your partner.

- What animals can you find in a zoo?
- Do you like visiting zoos? Why? / Why not?

2 Read the story. Who is Binti?

3 Read the story again and answer the questions.

1 How old was the child?
2 Which animals did he like best?
3 What happened when he was looking at the gorillas?
4 What did Binti do when the little boy fell into the enclosure?
5 What happened when the ambulance arrived?

GRAMMAR   Past simple and past continuous

4 Look at this sentence from the story and answer the questions.

> A
> *Binti was holding the little boy when the*
> B
> *ambulance arrived.*

1 Which verb is past simple, and which verb is past continuous?
2 Which action, **A** or **B**, started first?
3 Which action, **A** or **B**, interrupts the other?
→ Grammar reference **page 158**

5 Find two other sentences with *when* and *while* in the story. Answer the questions in Exercise 4 about them.

6 Find all other examples of the past simple and the past continuous in the text.

A lucky day

One day a three-year-old boy was visiting the zoo with his parents. He wanted to see all the animals but his favourites were the gorillas.

While the little boy was looking at the gorillas, suddenly he fell over the wall into their enclosure.

Binti, a female gorilla, was eating some fruit when the boy fell. She quickly picked him up and held him in her arms.

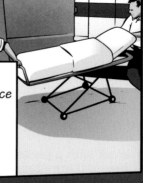

Binti was still holding the little boy when the ambulance arrived. She carried him to the door of the enclosure and the ambulance drove him to hospital.

7 Complete the sentences with one verb in the past simple and one in the past continuous.

0 The boy ...*was eating*... (eat) an ice cream when the bear ....*stole*......... (steal) it.

1 The cats .... (sleep) when the rain .... (start).

2 While the girl .... (read) a book, the chair .... (break).

3 The teacher .... (arrive) while Suzie and Tim .... (play) a computer game.

4 Wendy .... (eat) her lunch when her phone .... (ring).

5 The boy .... (fall off) his board while he .... (skate) in the park.

🎯 Corpus challenge

Can you find and correct the mistake here?
I enjoyed my holiday. I went to Larnaca. Every day, I was going swimming and after that, shopping.

SPEAKING

8 Look at the pictures below. Match the words to the pictures in the story. Some words match more than one picture.

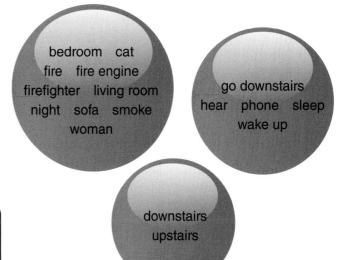

bedroom   cat   fire   fire engine   firefighter   living room   night   sofa   smoke   woman

go downstairs   hear   phone   sleep   wake up

downstairs   upstairs

9 Now tell the story with a partner. Use the past simple and the past continuous. Begin like this:

One night, Wendy was sleeping in her bed upstairs while Felix …

What can't these animals do!

VOCABULARY

1 Match the pictures of the animals to their names.

> bird   cat   dog   elephant   horse
> monkey   rabbit   rat   sheep

▶ 2.32 Listen and check.

2 Which of these animals can help people?
How do they help? What can they do?

READING

3 How can dogs be animal helpers? Look at
the pictures and discuss with your partner.

4 Dogs can do a lot to help people.
Read about these special dogs.
Choose the best word (A, B or C) for each space.

Most dogs are good (**0**) .... swimming but these dogs are very,
very good at it. They are dog lifeguards and they work on beaches in Italy
(**1**) .... the summer. They jump from helicopters and fast boats
(**2**) .... help people in danger in the water.

'Dogs don't get tired as quickly as we do,' says Emilio. 'A dog is strong and it
can (**3**) .... fast. It gets to a swimmer faster than we can and then
(**4**) .... pulls the person back to the beach.'

It takes three years to teach these dogs everything they (**5**) .... to
know. (**6**) .... they are ready to do their jobs.

0 A on	**B** (at)	**C** in
1 A during	**B** on	**C** since
2 A but	**B** or	**C** and
3 A swam	**B** swim	**C** swims
4 A it	**B** they	**C** you
5 A can	**B** need	**C** should
6 A When	**B** After	**C** Then

5 Work with a partner. Look at all the choices for Exercise 4 again.
How did you choose the correct answers?

LISTENING

6 ▶2.33 **Listen to the radio interview. What animal helper does Gary have? What's its name?**

7 ▶2.33 **Listen again. Are these sentences right (✔) or wrong (✗)?**

1 The show is called 'True Stories'.
2 The subject of this week's phone-in is 'animal helpers'.
3 Gary was cycling to work when a car hit him.
4 Gary read about animal helpers on the internet.
5 Gary's animal helper can open a drink for him.
6 Gary's animal helper is his best friend.

About you

8 What animals do people in your family have? Think about:

pets   animal helpers   farm animals

Share your ideas with your partner.

PRONUNCIATION   /uː/ and /ʊ/

9 ▶2.34 **Listen to the sounds /uː/ and /ʊ/. Look at the words and think about the sounds. Put them into the right column.**

| cook | good | food | look | moon |
| room | soon | tooth | wood | zoo |

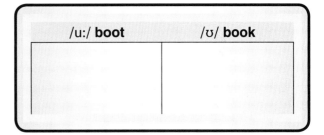

/uː/ **boot**	/ʊ/ **book**

▶2.35 **Listen and check. Then repeat.**

WRITING

Prepare to write – An email to a friend

GET READY Read this email from Joshua to his friend.

I've got a pet rabbit called Blackie. He's quite clever and can do tricks. My sister's pet is a cat called Sam. He's grey with a white nose. Both Sam and Blackie are very friendly. My granddad also likes animals but he prefers farm animals, for example sheep and chickens. He brings us eggs from his chickens every day. We don't have any animal helpers in our family. Write and tell me about the animals in your family.

• Look at the words in blue in Joshua's email. Complete these sentences with *both, also* and *for example*.

1 In my family, we've only got small pets, ... rats and mice.
2 My uncle's horse is brown with a white tail. It's .... got a white face.
3 I've got a dog and a rabbit. .... animals are white.

PLAN Makes notes about animals in your family. Use your ideas from Exercise 8.

WRITE Write a reply to Joshua in about 50 words about animals in your family. Use *both*, *also* and *for example* in your email.

IMPROVE Read your email and your partner's. Check for mistakes and give your partner two ideas to make their email better. Rewrite your email.

Geography
Tectonic plates and earthquakes

1 Look at the map of the world. Find where you live.

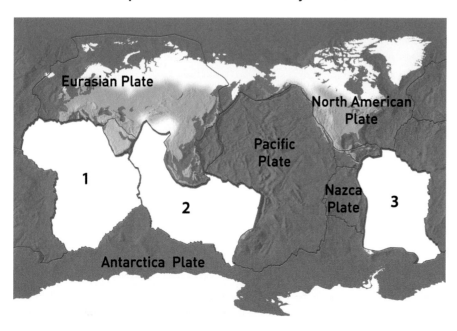

2 Read about tectonic plates. Then look at these three tectonic plates. Where do they go on the map above?

a Australian-Indian Plate   **b** South American Plate   **c** African Plate

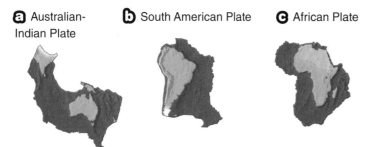

Tectonic plates

The outside surface of the Earth, the Earth's crust, is very thin and is made up of different pieces. We call these pieces tectonic plates. You can see some of the tectonic plates on the map, for example the Pacific Plate and the Nazca Plate. Underneath the tectonic plates there is molten rock called magma. Some of the plates, like the Pacific Plate, have an ocean on top of them.

3 Read and match the information to the correct picture.

a 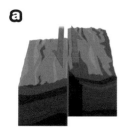   **b** 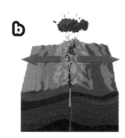   **c** 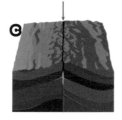   **d** 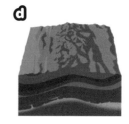   **e**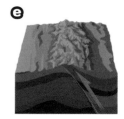

1 The tectonic plates float on top of the magma. They are not fixed. They can move.
2 The places where tectonic plates touch are called fault lines.
3 Sometimes the tectonic plates touch at these fault lines and move against each other. Then we have an earthquake.
4 Sometimes one tectonic plate moves over another plate and then mountains, for example the Himalayas, are formed.
5 Sometimes the tectonic plates move away from each other. When this happens, magma comes up to the surface of the Earth through a volcano.

4 Read about the San Andreas Fault. Then find it on the map in Exercise 1.

The San Andreas Fault

Some parts of the world have a lot of earthquakes because they are on a fault line. The San Andreas Fault in western California in the United States is probably the most famous fault line in the world. On land, it is more than a thousand kilometres long. It goes from just north of San Francisco to near the border with Mexico. The fault continues under the sea down the Gulf of California.

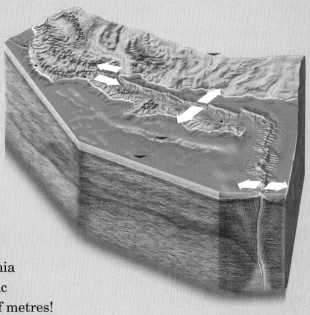

The San Andreas Fault is where two tectonic plates meet: the Pacific Plate and the North American Plate. The Pacific Plate is moving northwest against the North American Plate. The normal movement is about five centimetres a year and this slow movement does not cause earthquakes. But sometimes the plates get stuck against each other and cannot move. This can be dangerous because, when the plates start moving again, the movement can be very sudden and can release a lot of energy. This sudden movement of the two plates caused the big earthquake in California in 1906. The biggest movement of the Pacific Plate in that earthquake was six and a half metres!

5 Read the text again. Then find these numbers in the text and tell your partner what they are.

1 1906   **2** 5   **3** 6.5   **4** 1,000   **5** 2

6 Look at the pictures for the earthquake drill in California.

① DROP!   ② COVER!   ③ HOLD ON!

Protect Yourself. Spread The Word

Now match the verbs to the rest of the sentences to complete the drill.

1 Drop   **a** until the shaking stops.
2 Take cover   **b** to something.
3 Hold on   **c** under a desk or table.

Project — Make a poster

Work in groups.
The Ring of Fire is a large area around the edge of the Pacific Ocean where there are a lot of earthquakes and volcanoes.

Use the internet or books to find out:
- where the Ring of Fire is
- the names of countries it passes through
- the names of some of the volcanoes on the Ring of Fire
- when there were volcanic eruptions and earthquakes on the Ring of Fire

Make a poster to show what you know about the Ring of Fire.

Review 4

Units 13–16

VOCABULARY

1 **Find the odd word out in each set. Say why it does not fit.**

0	lake	(cloudy)	mountain	forest
1	duck	monkey	castle	rabbit
2	library	forest	supermarket	restaurant
3	race	headache	temperature	pain
4	helicopter	bicycle	bus	roundabout
5	deep	left	wide	high

2 **Read the descriptions of some words. Find the word and write the missing letters.**

0 When the weather is like this, it's difficult to see where you're going. s _ _ e _
1 This has a blue light and can make a loud noise when it takes people to hospital. f o g g y
2 If you're ill, you can take this to help you feel better. a _ _ u _ _ _ c _
3 We get wool and meat from this farm animal. m _ _ _ c _ n _
4 When this happens, there's a lot of noise, rain and wind. ex _ _ _ i _ e
5 Doing lots of this keeps you healthy. t _ _ _ d _ _ s _ _ _ m

GRAMMAR

3 **◉ Choose the right word to complete the sentences.**

1 I ate with my family *out / outside* the tent.
2 It's very easy to get to the sports centre because it's *in front of / opposite* my house.
3 I took a trip *through / down* the River Nile.
4 You *shall / should* bring some of your computer games.

◉ Correct the mistakes in these sentences.

5 I enjoyed my holiday. Every day I was going swimming.
6 I liked the tennis match because were playing Nadal and Loranzo.
7 In Thailand, I visited many places and the most interesting thing is eating the food there.
8 In Taipei it was raining when we got there.

4 **Complete the sentences with the verb in brackets. Use the past simple or past continuous.**

0 It ...*wasn't raining*.. (not rain) when I ....*left*............ (leave) the house this morning.
1 When I .... (arrive) at the party, my friend .... (sing) in the living room.
2 I .... (walk) around the shops when I .... (meet) my friend.
3 My dad .... (call) me while I .... (do) my homework.
4 I .... (not run) when I .... (hurt) my foot. I .... (dance).
5 I .... (not see) any animals when I .... (walk) in the forest.

5 **Give these people some advice, using *should* or *shouldn't*.**

0 I've got a temperature and a headache.
   You should take some medicine and go to bed. / You shouldn't go to school.
1 My running shoes are too small.
2 I really want a pet!
3 The weather's really hot and I want to go to the beach.
4 I've got nothing to wear to my friend's party.
5 I don't know the way to the museum.

WRITING

6 Read the advertisement and the email. Fill in the information in Kelly's notes.

Star Cinema

Saturday and Sunday
2 pm and 8 pm

Screen 1 **Monkey Man**
Screen 2 **Red Mountain**

Tickets

Children (under 15) - **£6.00**
Adults - **£8.50**

Book online at www.starcinema.com

From:	Sasha
To:	Kelly

About our cinema trip on Saturday – Mum says I have to go in the afternoon, I'm afraid! And can you get three tickets instead of two? My cousin wants to come with us. She saw *Monkey Man* last Sunday, so we'll have to see the other film. Hope that's OK! She's 13 by the way, like us.

Kelly's notes
Cinema trip

Website address: **0** *www.starcinema.com*
Number of tickets to book: **1** ....
Name of film: **2** ....
Day: **3** ....
Time: **4** .... *pm*
Price per person: **5** £ ....

LISTENING

7 ▶ 2.36 Listen to a boy, Dominic, telling his friend about a visit to a theme park. Choose the right answer.

1 How much did Dominic pay for his ticket?

A    B

2 What was the weather like?

A    B

3 How many rides did Dominic go on?

A **3**   B **4**

4 Which animals did Dominic see?

A    B

SPEAKING

8 Put the words in the right order to make questions.

1 feeling / how / you / today / are / ?
2 your / animal / favourite / what's / ?
3 weather / today / what's / like / the / ?
4 do / like / you / countryside / in / doing / what / the / ?

Ask and answer the questions with your partner. Take turns to speak.

9 Now talk about where you live. Take turns to speak.

Tell me about where you live.

I live in a small town. There's a park near the …

17 What's on?
I'm going to record it

VOCABULARY

1 Check the meaning of the words in blue in your dictionary.

1 Which TV channel do you usually watch?

2 Which TV programmes are you a big fan of?

3 Do you ever record TV programmes? Which ones? Why?

4 What did you watch on TV last night?

5 Do you watch cartoons? Which ones do you like?

▶2.37 Listen and repeat the words in blue.

LISTENING

3 ▶2.38 Listen. Mina and Clyde meet in the street. What does Clyde invite Mina to do?

4 ▶2.38 Listen again and answer the questions.

1 When is the concert?

2 What is the name of the band?

3 Which channel does Mina think the concert is on?

4 Did Mina want to go to the concert?

5 Why does Mina want to watch the concert at Paula's house?

6 Who has got tickets for the concert?

7 Who do you think likes the band more, Clyde or Mina?

About you

2 Ask and answer the questions in Exercise 1 with your partner.

GRAMMAR Future with *going to*

5 Look at the table and then complete the sentences. Use words from the table.

I'm (I am)	I'm not		
He's (He is)	He isn't		
She's (She is)	She isn't	going to	watch the concert on TV.
We're (We are)	We aren't		go to the concert.
You're (You are)	You aren't		
They're (They are)	They aren't		

→ Grammar reference **page 159**

1 Mina and Clyde (not) ....

2 Paula ....

3 Anita (not) ....

4 Mina and Clyde ....

6 Mina was talking to Clyde about her *plans* for next Saturday.

1 Which picture, a) or b), shows her plans *before* her conversation with Clyde?

2 Which picture, a) or b), shows her plans *after* her conversation with Clyde?

7 Complete the sentence.

We can use *(not) going to* + the .... to talk about future plans.

8 Complete the speech bubbles. Use *going to*.

Sorry, Clyde, I can't. I'm …
We're …

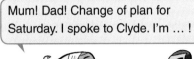

Mum! Dad! Change of plan for Saturday. I spoke to Clyde. I'm … !

9 Paula (P) and Anita (A) are going to watch The Rock Sisters' concert on TV. Look at their list and write what they are *going to* or *not going to* do.

Buy pizzas and lemonade P & A
~~Phone my friend Clara~~ P
~~Make a cake?~~ A
Bring chocolate A
Invite Ruby P
Tell my mum and dad A
Record the concert P
~~Invite Nick and Eddie~~ A & P

Paula and Anita are going to buy pizzas and lemonade.
Paula isn't going to phone her friend Clara.

Corpus challenge

Can you correct this sentence?
We are going play tennis at the sports centre.

PRONUNCIATION *going to*

10 ▶2.39 Listen and repeat.

Now read your answers to Exercise 9 to your partner.

EP Get talking! → page 128

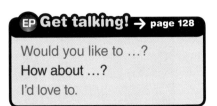

Would you like to …?
How about …?
I'd love to.

SPEAKING

11 Work in groups. Ask and answer. Look at the times below and talk about your plans.

Say some things you're going to do and some things you're not going to do.

A: *What are you going to do next Sunday afternoon?*
B: *I'm going to visit my granny and granddad. I'm not going to do any homework!*

this evening **next summer**

next Saturday morning

tomorrow morning

next Sunday afternoon

when you're 18

What's your favourite TV show?

READING AND VOCABULARY

1 Look at the pictures. What do you know about these TV shows?

2 Read the questions and talk about your ideas with your partner.
- Are the people on the show actors or real people?
- What different kinds of talent show are there?
- Who chooses the winners?
- What do winners of talent shows get?

3 Read the text quickly and check your ideas. Put a question from Exercise 2 into each space.

TALENT SHOWS

What do you really know about talent shows?

Everyone knows *The X Factor*! It's a talent show for people who want to become famous singers. A few people on the show are excellent singers but a lot of them aren't! There are lots of other shows around the world as well. In many countries, they are the most popular shows on TV.

1 ....
There are shows for musicians, people doing magic, singers and dancers … and some national talent shows for singing dogs and robots too!

2 ....
I'm sure you know the answer to this one. Usually, the people watching the show on TV and in the theatre choose who (or what!) they like best. Sometimes famous people choose as well. And the winners aren't always good-looking.

3 ....
They are competitions, so there is always a winner. Sometimes the winner gets money, sometimes they get a recording contract and become stars. On a few shows, they get nothing – but they are famous!

4 ....
Most of the time they're real people– if they're not robots or dogs, that is! But the people don't always choose what they want to say. On some shows, there's an autocue. This tells people the words they must say. They're a bit like actors in a play!

4 Complete the sentences with the words in the box.

> competition   excellent   good-looking
> national   stage   star   theatre

1 She's the best dancer. I want her to win the ....
2 There were eight singers on a small .... It was very crowded!
3 We went to see the concert in a very big ....
4 He won a talent show four years ago. Now he's a big ....
5 It's a .... show. It's only for people from the UK.
6 He wasn't .... but he could sing really well.
7 I like *The X Factor*. Every show is .... !

5 ▶2.41 **Listen to Sandra talking to her friend Ben about *The X Factor*.**
Did Sandra and Ben like the same singers on the show?

6 ▶2.41 **Listen again. Choose the right picture for each question.**

1 Who did Sandra like?

2 Who did Ben like?

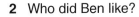

VOCABULARY   Describing people

7 **Complete Sandra's description. Then write Ben's description.**

He's got .... brown .... and lovely .... eyes.
He's quite .... and ....
He was wearing black .... and a blue ....
He's really ....

8 **Describe the two people in the picture. Use the words in the box and the verbs in the word map to help you.**

attractive   beautiful   blonde   dark   fair
good-looking   old   pretty   short   slim
tall   young

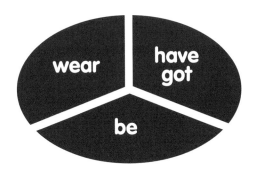

9 Think about these questions.
  • Do you have talent shows in your country?
  • What are they called?
  • Do you like them? Why? / Why not?
  • Can you name some of the actors or some famous winners? Are they stars?
  • Would you like to be in a competition like *The X Factor*? Why? / Why not?
  • Do you think it's more important to be a good singer or to be good-looking to win these competitions?

  Now discuss your answers with your partner.

WRITING

10 **Work with a partner. Choose a TV show you both like.**

Make notes about the show and about one of the actors or stars.

11 **Write 25–30 words about the show. Describe one of the winners or one of your favourite actors on the show.**

Use the text in Exercise 3 and your answers to Exercises 7 and 8 to help you.

18 Papers and magazines
Let's think of some ideas

VOCABULARY

1 Match the words to the pictures.

> advertisement   cartoon   magazine
> newspaper   notice

▶ 2.42 Listen and check. Then repeat.

2 Discuss the questions in groups.

- Do you have a school magazine or newspaper?
- What's it called?
- What's in your school magazine or newspaper?
- If you don't have a school magazine or newspaper, what would you like to include in one?

a Daily News
Euro crisis throws brakes on lending

Egypt takes historic turn at voting booth

b

c No football practice tonight
Mr Smith is ill

d Looking for a new phone?

We've got the best offers
Click here ▶

e New Movies this summer   FREE booklet!
TEENZ
NEW
FASHION ALERT
New looks this month
STAR SCOOP
Good goes bad
High School Music drama!
the best summer beauty tricks

LISTENING

3 ▶ 2.43 Listen to Jack, Molly and Ravi. They're making plans for their school magazine. What's Jack going to do after the meeting?

4 ▶ 2.43 Listen again. Tick (✔) the things the friends want to include in their magazine.

advertisements ☐
book reviews ☐
cartoons ☐
film reviews ☐
information about the school ☐
music reviews ☐
photos ☐
play reviews ☐
stories ☐
website addresses ☐

GRAMMAR   Making suggestions

A suggestion is a plan or idea that you want someone to think about.
Look at the examples from the recording. The words in red are different ways of making suggestions.

- **Why don't** we write down some ideas now?
- **Let's** have some stories too.
- **Shall** we include advertisements?
- **Why not** ask your dad about it?

→ **Grammar reference** page 160

5 **Put the words in the right order to make suggestions.**

Add a full stop or a question mark and start the sentence with a capital letter.

1 we / don't / go / to / cinema / why / the
2 the / new / see / let's / cartoon / Japanese
3 ask / come / Mina / why / to / not
4 meet / we / there / at / shall / eight

▶2.44 **Listen and check. Then repeat.**

6 **Complete the conversation. Use each phrase from the Grammar box once. There is often more than one right answer.**

Ravi: I think we need some more help with the magazine.

Molly: You're right. (**1**) .... ask our teacher to help? Is that a good idea?

Ravi: No, I don't think so. She's very busy. I can write a note and give it to all the teachers.

Molly: No, that's not a good idea. We want students to see it, too. (**2**) .... put a notice on the school website.

Ravi: Excellent idea.

Molly: (**3**) .... write it now?

Ravi: OK. *Magazine helpers wanted!*

Molly: Great! (**4**) .... write our names at the bottom?

Ravi: Good idea. OK, let's write it on the computer now!

Corpus challenge

Can you correct this sentence? Choose the right answer.

~~Lets~~ go to a restaurant and eat some pizza after the film.
A Shall   **B** Why don't   **C** Let's

PRONUNCIATION   Intonation

7 ▶2.45 **Listen and repeat these phrases from the conversations about the magazine.**

No, that's not a good idea.   Cool!
No, I don't think so.   Sounds good!
Great!   Good one!
OK.   You're right!
                                    Excellent idea.

8 **Practise the conversation in Exercise 6 with a partner.**

SPEAKING

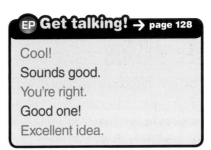

EP Get talking! → page 128

Cool!
Sounds good.
You're right.
Good one!
Excellent idea.

9 **Work in groups of four. Plan a class magazine. Use your ideas from Exercise 2 to help you.**

1 Make suggestions to the group.
  Listen to suggestions and say what you think.
  Agree a list of two ideas.

2 Tell your ideas to another group.
  Listen to their ideas.
  Agree a list of four ideas.

3 Tell your ideas to the class.
  Listen to other groups' ideas.
  Agree a list of six ideas.

You should read it!

READING

1 Look at pictures. One is a film poster, the other is a book cover. Do you know these stories?

What do you think the film *School of Rock* is about?

What do you think the book *Charlie and the Chocolate Factory* is about?

2 Read these reviews and check your ideas.

School of Rock

School of Rock is about a guitar player called Dewey Finn. He leaves his band because the band members don't want him to play with them any more. But then he doesn't have any money so he looks for a job. When he gets a job as a teacher in a school, the students really like him. They think he's funny and a little bit mad! Dewey decides to start a rock band as there are lots of good musicians in his class. He enters a competition called 'Battle of the Bands' with his new school band and – do they win? Why don't you see the film and find out!

It's quite an old film but I saw it on DVD last week. I really loved it. Jack Black plays Dewey Finn and he's great and really funny. Make sure you see it one day!

Charlie AND THE CHOCOLATE FACTORY

Charlie Bucket lives in a small house with his parents and grandparents. They're very poor. One day Charlie finds some money on the street and he decides to buy a Wonka chocolate bar with it. When he opens the chocolate bar, Charlie finds a golden ticket inside. It's his lucky day! It's a ticket to visit Willy Wonka's famous Chocolate Factory. Charlie is very excited. Grandpa Joe is excited too, because he goes on the visit with Charlie. As there are five golden tickets, four other children visit the factory as well. First they all meet Willy Wonka, who's a bit mad. Then they go around the factory. Lots of strange things happen! Only Charlie is left at the end, so he's the winner! What's the prize? Why not read the book and find out?

This book is very funny and the story is exciting. If you like Johnny Depp, watch the film too. He's Willy Wonka!

3 Read the reviews again and answer the questions.

1 Why does Dewey Finn leave the band?
2 Where does he get a job?
3 What do the students think of him?
4 What's 'Battle of the Bands'?
5 Did the writer like the film?
6 Where does Charlie get the money for the chocolate bar?
7 Who is Willy Wonka?
8 Who goes with Charlie to the factory?
9 How many golden tickets are there?
10 Who wins the prize at the end?
11 What is the prize?
12 Did the writer like the book?

4 Which parts of the reviews *tell the story* of the film or book and which parts are the writers' *opinions*?

VOCABULARY   as, because, so, when

5 Look at the reviews again. We use the words in blue to connect ideas in sentences.

Match the sentence halves.

1 Dewey Finn left his band
2 Dewey decided to start a rock band
3 When he opened the chocolate bar,

4 Charlie was left at the end

a so he was the winner.
b as there were lots of good musicians in his class.
c because the other musicians didn't want to play with him any more.
d Charlie found a golden ticket inside.

6 Complete the review of the play with the words in blue from Exercise 5.

Romeo and Juliet
by Shakespeare

Romeo and Juliet is a really sad story about two young people. Their families don't want them to marry **(1)** .... the families hate each other. However, Romeo and Juliet are in love and they get married. They know their families will be very angry, **(2)** .... they don't tell them!

Juliet's family don't know she's married and they find a husband for her. But she can't marry this man **(3)** .... she's already married to Romeo. Juliet is very unhappy. She drinks something and goes to sleep. **(4)** .... Romeo finds Juliet, he thinks she is dead. He kills himself. But Juliet isn't dead! She wakes up, sees Romeo is dead and kills herself. And that's the end!

I saw the play at the City Theatre. The actors were all great and I cried at the end. I loved it. Go and see it.

LISTENING

7 ▶2.47 Molly, Jack and Ravi are trying to choose one of the three reviews for the magazine. Which one does each of them like?

8 ▶2.47 Listen again. Write the reasons for their choices.

About you

9 Think about a film, play or book that you like. Make notes.

Tell your partner the story and give your opinion.

The book is called 'Harry Potter and the Goblet of Fire'. It's about a boy …

It's a very good book. I loved it. You should read it!

WRITING

Prepare to write — A review

GET READY You're going to write a review. Read the three reviews in Exercises 2 and 6 again and look at your notes from Exercise 9.

PLAN Plan your review.

WRITE Write a review of a film, a play or a book in about 50 words. Try to use *as, because, so, when*.

IMPROVE Read your review and your partner's. Check for mistakes. Give your partner three ideas to make their review better. Rewrite your review and give it to your teacher for the class magazine.

Culture
An island in the sun

1 Look at the pictures of this 'island in the sun'. What's the country called? What do you know about it?

Caribbean Sea

2 Quickly read some fun facts about the island on the opposite page.

Match six of the facts 1–8 to the six pictures a–f.

3 Read the fun facts again. Are the sentences right (✔) or wrong (✘)?

1 Bananas are part of the national dish.
2 The film *Cool Runnings* is about Usain Bolt.
3 The giant swallowtail is a butterfly.
4 People on the island say 'Out of many, one people'.
5 Bob Marley is an athlete.
6 The country sends a team to the Winter Olympics.

4 ▶2.48 Listen to four pieces of music. Which one is reggae?

5 Discuss the questions.

1 What music is typical of your country?
2 What are the names of some musicians from your country?
3 What are the names of some sports people from your country?
4 What is your country famous for?
5 What do farmers grow in your country?
6 What wild animals are there?
7 What is your national dish?

FUN FACTS

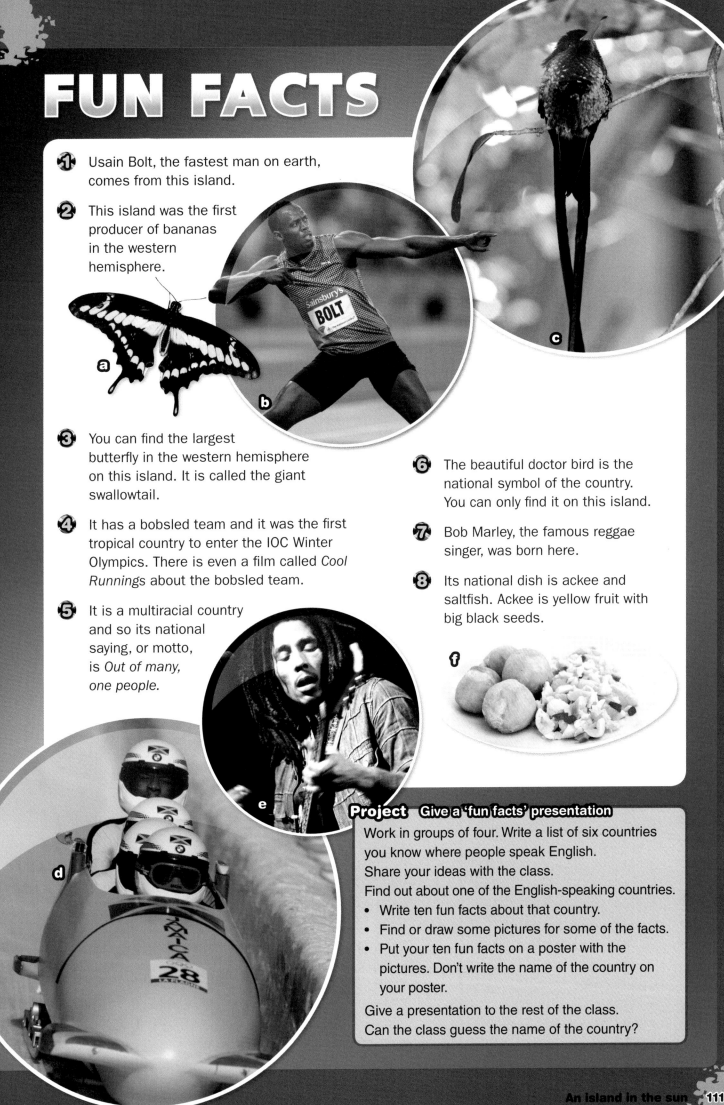

1. Usain Bolt, the fastest man on earth, comes from this island.

2. This island was the first producer of bananas in the western hemisphere.

3. You can find the largest butterfly in the western hemisphere on this island. It is called the giant swallowtail.

4. It has a bobsled team and it was the first tropical country to enter the IOC Winter Olympics. There is even a film called *Cool Runnings* about the bobsled team.

5. It is a multiracial country and so its national saying, or motto, is *Out of many, one people.*

6. The beautiful doctor bird is the national symbol of the country. You can only find it on this island.

7. Bob Marley, the famous reggae singer, was born here.

8. Its national dish is ackee and saltfish. Ackee is yellow fruit with big black seeds.

Project   Give a 'fun facts' presentation

Work in groups of four. Write a list of six countries you know where people speak English.
Share your ideas with the class.
Find out about one of the English-speaking countries.
- Write ten fun facts about that country.
- Find or draw some pictures for some of the facts.
- Put your ten fun facts on a poster with the pictures. Don't write the name of the country on your poster.

Give a presentation to the rest of the class.
Can the class guess the name of the country?

19 School can be fun!
Do we have to wear our uniform?

End-of-term school trip for year 8
Tall Trees Activity Camp

Cost: £200

Dates: 25th–28th July
If you want to go, pay Miss Smith by (1) .... July.
The bus leaves school at 8.30 am on 25th July. But be there
at (2) .... am. Don't be late!

For the journey:
Please wear school uniform.
You don't need to bring snacks or (3) ....
Bring a (4) ....

What to pack:
For swimming – a towel and a (5) ....
For other outdoor activities – old trainers and old
(6) ....

For the disco – some nice (7) ....

1 Read the information about
the school trip and look at the
pictures. Answer the questions
in groups.
- What activities can you see
in the pictures?
- Do you do activities like
these on school trips?
- Which of these activities
would you like to do?
- Which ones wouldn't you like
to do?
- What did you do on your last
school trip?

VOCABULARY

2 Match the words to their meanings.

1 activity   **a** This is the price of something.
2 term   **b** This is when you travel from one place to
     another.
3 disco   **c** This is something you do, often for fun.
4 uniform   **d** You do this when you put things into a
     suitcase.
5 journey   **e** You go here to dance.
6 pack   **f** People wear this at school or in a job, so
     everyone looks the same.
7 towel   **g** You dry yourself with this after washing or
     swimming.
8 cost   **h** In Britain, this is about 12 weeks long, and
     there are three of them in the school year.

LISTENING

3 ▶2.49 **Listen to Annika asking Harry for some information about the school trip and answer the questions.**

1 Why wasn't Annika at the school meeting?
2 Where's the activity centre?
3 As well as swimming, what other outdoor activities can they do?
4 What are Annika and Harry going to do this afternoon?

4 ▶2.49 **Listen again and complete the note from school on the opposite page.**

GRAMMAR   *have to / don't have to*

5 **Match the two halves of the sentences.**

1 We *have to be* at school
2 Mr Peters *has to check*
3 We *have to bring* some nice clothes
4 We *don't have to bring* snacks
5 I *don't have to go* shopping
6 *Do we have to wear*

a or drinks with us.
b to wear.
c because I've got everything I need.
d our names.
e our school uniform?
f at eight o'clock.

→ Grammar reference **page 161**

Now read the examples and answer the questions.

> We have to be at school at eight o'clock.

> I don't have to go shopping.

Can they come to school at 8.30?

Can she go shopping if she wants to?

6 **Complete the table.**

Obligation	No obligation	Question form
I/you/we/they have to go	I/you/we/they _____ go	_____ I/you/we/they _____ go?
he/she/it _____ go	he/she/it doesn't have to go	Does he/she/it have to go?

7 ▶2.50 **Listen to Dillon asking about the school trip. Tick (✔) the things he has to do.**

get up early every day ☐
go climbing ☐
go sailing ☐
go to the disco ☐
leave his phone at home ☐
share a bedroom ☐
help with the cleaning ☐
do any school work ☐

Corpus challenge

Can you see what's wrong with this sentence? Add two words.
You don't bring anything – it's not necessary.

PRONUNCIATION   *have to / has to*

8 ▶2.51 **Listen and repeat.**

9 **Ask and answer about the things in Exercise 7 with a partner.**

> Does Dillon have to get up early every day?

> Yes, he does.

SPEAKING

10 **Work with a partner. Ask and answer about what you have to do / don't have to do this weekend. Use these ideas or your own.**

visit anyone?   go shopping?
do any homework?   do any cleaning?
get up early?   go to bed early?

Do you have to visit anyone this weekend?
Yes, I do. / No, I don't.

School can be fun!   **113**

They don't have to study

A DIFFERENT WAY TO LEARN

Manor Park School in California has a gym, ten classrooms, a library and a kitchen. However, there are no timetables, no homework and no exams. Teachers don't give students marks for their work and they never give them tests. There are lessons but students don't have to go to them. They can choose what they do and how they spend their time. If they don't want to study, they can play video games, talk with friends or watch TV. They can cook a meal if they're hungry, or bring food from home and eat it when they like.

If students want to do a project or learn something, they can ask for lessons. Anyone can go to these classes, from the youngest student, who is five, to the oldest students, who are 18. Often students teach the classes themselves. Thirteen-year-old Lewis taught a class on cosmology to a group of older students last week. He says he's very interested in space and reads a lot about it. He's going to give more classes over the next few weeks.

Other subjects available at the moment are Chinese, nature study, maths, bike repair, film-making, art, music and photography. The head teacher says it's not very important for children to learn hard things like chemistry or physics. 'They just forget it,' she says. 'Instead, they need to learn how to learn. Then, when they're interested in something, they know how to find out about it by themselves.'

READING AND VOCABULARY

1 Read the text about the Manor Park School. Are these sentences right (A) or wrong (B)?

1 Students at the school don't have to study.   **A B**
2 Teachers tell students what they have to do every day.   **A B**
3 Students of all ages can study together.   **A B**
4 Lewis has to teach one class a week.   **A B**
5 The head teacher thinks students should study chemistry.   **A B**
6 The head teacher thinks students can learn without a teacher.   **A B**

2 Read the text again. Complete the table for Manor Park School with vocabulary from the text. Then think about your own school and add more words to each column.

	Places	People	Subjects	Things students do	Things teachers do
Manor Park	gym	teacher	cosmology	play video games	give lessons
My school					

SPEAKING

3 Work in groups. Discuss the sentences.

- I'd like to go to a school like Manor Park.
- I like getting marks for my work.
- Tests and exams are important.
- Bike repair and film-making are more useful than chemistry and physics.

LISTENING

4 ▶2.52 Alice goes to a boarding school. She sleeps there and only goes home for holidays. Listen to her describing her school. Number the pictures as you listen.

5 Alice wrote this article about her school for the TV programme website. Can you fill in any of the spaces?

> I go to a boarding school called Hartland School. It has about **(1)** .... pupils.
>
> I have to share a bedroom with **(2)** .... other girls. We can put **(3)** .... of our family on the walls.
>
> There's a library where we do our homework. We start at **(4)** .... every night. We work really hard at my school. We even have lessons on **(5)** .... mornings! After homework, we can go to the **(6)** .... room to have some fun.
>
> We have meals in a big **(7)** .... and we have to help with the **(8)** .... afterwards.
>
> We have to do sports at my school. Next term, we're going to do **(9)** ....

▶2.52 **Listen again to check.**

6 Write four pairs of sentences to compare Hartland School and Manor Park School. Use *have to / don't have to* and *can/can't*.

At Hartland School, students have to eat together. At Manor Park School, students can eat when they want.

WRITING

7 Write an article about your perfect school. Plan before you write. Think about:

- a name for your school
- the size of your school
- what students can/can't do
- what students have to / don't have to do
- what the teachers are like
- what subjects you study

8 Read some of your classmates' articles. Can you guess who wrote them?

20 Families
Her family worked hard

READING AND VOCABULARY

1 Read about Kate's family. Complete her family tree with people's names.

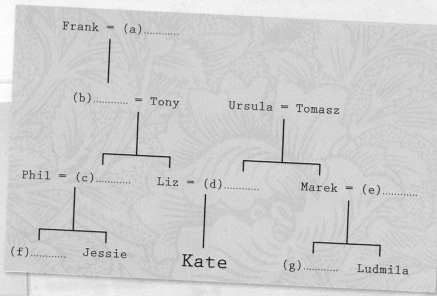

Frank = (a)...........

(b)........... = Tony   Ursula = Tomasz

Phil = (c)...........   Liz = (d)...........   Marek = (e)...........

(f)........... Jessie   Kate   (g)........... Ludmila

My family tree

My name's Kate and this is my family tree. My mother is English and my father is Polish. His name is Wiktor and all his family live in Poland, so I go there quite often. I know a bit of Polish but when people speak fast, I can't understand them! I stay with my grandparents, my Uncle Marek, his wife Kasia and my two cousins, Jana and Ludmila. Jana plays the piano really well and Ludmila is good at chess. She wins easily every time we play!

My mother's name is Liz. Her sister, Helen, is married to Phil and they have two small children – a son called Oliver and a daughter called Jessie. They're very sweet but very noisy! My granny is called Sue and she grew up in South Africa. That's where she met my grandpa, Tony.

Granny often tells me stories about her mother – my great-grandmother. She was called Iris and she was born in 1910 on a small farm in South Africa. She was very musical and loved singing. Her family worked hard and sent her to England to study music. She became a singer and sang in some of the most famous theatres in London. Granny has a big box of old photographs of her. I love looking at them but I have to hold them carefully because they're very old. Granny's trying to find out about Iris's parents and grandparents now. I'm sure there are lots more interesting stories in my family history.

2 Put the family words into the right column of the table.

aunt   brother   child/children   cousin   daughter   father   grandchild   granddaughter   grandfather   grandmother   grandparent   grandson   mother   sister   son   uncle

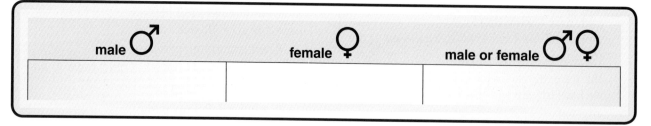

male ♂	female ♀	male or female ♂♀

▶ 2.53 **Listen and check. Then repeat.**

3 Make eight sentences about Kate's family tree. Compare with a partner. Are any of your sentences the same?

Tony is Jessie's grandfather.   *Marek is Jana and Ludmila's dad.*

GRAMMAR   Adverbs of manner

4 Read the text again and think about the words in red. These are adverbs of manner. Choose the right word to complete the sentences.

> 1 Adverbs of manner describe *how* / *when* we do things.
> 2 We make *many* / *all* adverbs of manner by adding *-ly* to an adjective.

→ Grammar reference **page 162**

5 Find three adverbs in the text that do not end with *-ly*. Write their adjectives.

6 Look at the spelling rules below, then write the adverbs for the adjectives.

> | bad | easy | loud | noisy |
> | quick | quiet | slow | wonderful |

> **Spelling rules for making *-ly* adverbs**
> | Adjective | Adverb |
> |---|---|
> | slow | slowly (add -ly) |
> | happy | happily |
> | | (change y to i) |
> | careful | carefully |
> | | (double the l) |

7 Make adverbs from the adjectives in the box. Use them to complete the sentences. Then ask and answer with a partner.

> | careful | easy | fast | good | hard |
> | loud | noisy | quick | quiet | slow |

1 Do you always do your homework .... ?
2 Can you run .... ?
3 Can you sing .... ?
4 Do you speak .... on the bus?
5 Do you play music .... ?
6 Can you make friends .... ?

⊘ Corpus challenge

Can you correct this sentence?
I liked the competition because both teams played very good.

PRONUNATION   The letter *i*

8 Work with a partner. What sound does *i* make in the words? Put them into the right column.

> | child | children | find | history | interesting |
> | kind | quickly | quietly | quite | sing |

> | /ɪ/ **milk** | /aɪ/ **night** |
> |---|---|
> | | |

▶ 2.54 Listen and check. Repeat the words.

READING

9 Choose the right word to complete the sentences.

0 Every family ...B... lots of interesting stories in its past.
   A does   **B** (has)   **C** is
1 It's not too .... to find out about your family history.
   A busy   **B** difficult   **C** long
2 First you should .... older family members about their parents and grandparents.
   A talk   **B** say   **C** ask
3 Listen .... and write down what they tell you.
   A carefully   **B** easily   **C** quickly
4 The first .... you need to find out is when and where people were born.
   A place   **B** thing   **C** person
5 Check your information is .... because you don't want mistakes in your family tree.
   A correct   **B** normal   **C** full

SPEAKING

About you

10 Complete the table about your family. Under 'extra information', put an adjective (e.g. *clever*) or a verb plus adverb (e.g. *sings badly*) or an interesting fact (e.g. *grew up in China*).

Family member	Relationship to me	Extra information

11 Work in groups. Tell each other about the people in your table.

Mother's Day is especially important

READING

1 Read the newspaper article about a large family. Are the sentences right (A) or wrong (B)? If there isn't enough information to answer right or wrong, choose C (Doesn't say).

Hannah Dexter is 14 years old and belongs to a very large family. She has 17 brothers and sisters. As she is one of the older children, she has to help her parents a lot. 'I have to work quite hard,' she says, 'but I don't mind. I feel lucky to be in such a big family.'

The family lives in a six-bedroom house. The children sleep in triple bunk beds and everyone's clothes are in a special room downstairs, as there isn't space for cupboards in their bedrooms.

Hannah says the mornings are really busy. She and her older brothers and sisters work together to get the younger children ready for school. Every day for breakfast, the family needs nearly four litres of milk, two-and-a-half boxes of cereal and almost three loaves of bread.

A normal family car isn't big enough for the Dexters, so they have a mini-bus with 20 seats instead. And when they go on holiday, it's always camping. They have a 20-man tent that the whole family can sleep in quite comfortably.

A REALLY **BIG** FAMILY

Mother's Day is important in every family but for Hannah's family, it's especially important. It's the only day of the year when Hannah's mum can rest and do nothing. The children give her cards and presents and look after her all day. They make it as perfect for her as they possibly can.

0 There are 15 children in Hannah Dexter's family.
   A Right   **B** Wrong   **C** Doesn't say

1 Hannah is happy to be in a big family.
   A Right   **B** Wrong   **C** Doesn't say

2 The children keep their clothes in cupboards in their bedrooms.
   A Right   **B** Wrong   **C** Doesn't say

3 Hannah's dad leaves the house before the children go to school.
   A Right   **B** Wrong   **C** Doesn't say

4 The family eats the same things for breakfast every day.
   A Right   **B** Wrong   **C** Doesn't say

5 The Dexters got their mini-van two years ago.
   A Right   **B** Wrong   **C** Doesn't say

6 There are a few days every year when Hannah's mum does nothing.
   A Right   **B** Wrong   **C** Doesn't say

7 Hannah and her brothers and sisters try hard to make Mother's Day special for their mum.
   A Right   **B** Wrong   **C** Doesn't say

Compare your answers with a partner.

VOCABULARY   Adverbs of degree

2 Find the adverbs in the article.

> really   quite   especially   nearly   almost

1 Which two mean 'very much'?
2 Which two mean 'very close to'?
3 Which one means 'not completely'?

3 Complete each sentence with a different adverb from Exercise 2. Sometimes more than one is possible.

1 Sally's my best friend. I .... like her.
2 In my family, we all eat dinner together .... every night.
3 I like all my teachers, ... my English teacher.
4 I'm not sure about this colour. It's .... nice, I suppose.
5 Can you wait for me for five minutes? I'm .... ready.

SPEAKING

4 Ask and answer in groups.

- How many children are there in your family?
- Talk about the biggest family you know. How many children are in the family?
- Do you have Mother's Day in your country? What do you do?

LISTENING

5 ▶ 2.55 **Listen to three young people talking about who they live with. Match each speaker to the right picture.**

Shami

Sally

Harry

① ② ③

6 ▶ 2.55 **Listen again. Who's this? Write Shami, Sally or Harry next to each sentence.**

1 I live with one of my grandparents.
2 I have to travel quite a long way to see my dad.
3 My sister is still single.
4 I don't spend a lot of time with my cousins.
5 My brother and I sleep in the same room.
6 There are two families in my home.

WRITING

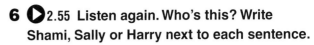

GET READY Read Sally's description of her family. Underline *also*, *too* and *as well*.

> *I live with my parents in a three-bedroom house. I'm the only child in my family — I haven't got any brothers or sisters. My grandfather lives with us as well. He's 78, and he's got lots of interesting stories to tell. I've also got four cousins and I like spending time with them too. They're the same age as me but I don't see them very often, because they live quite far away.*

Look at these examples and the ones in Sally's description and complete the rules below.

> My uncle lives on our street **as well**.
> My cousin likes it **too**.
> My sister is **also** getting married.
> I **also** spend time with my dad.

1 *Too* and *as well* go at the .... of the sentence.
2 *Also* goes <u>after</u> *be* and *have* but .... other verbs.

PLAN Make notes about your family.

WRITE Write a description of your family in about 50–60 words. Use *too*, *also* and *as well*.

IMPROVE Read your description and your partner's. Correct any mistakes, especially with *too*, *also* and *as well*, and rewrite it.

Biology
Animals and their habitats

1 How many animals can you name in English? How many parts of an animal's body can you name?

2 Read the information about animals and their habitats. Find these things in the pictures.

| claws | eyelashes | fur | hump | skin | teeth | trunk | tusk |

Animals and their habitats

Animals are able to live all over the world, in many different kinds of habitat. Some habitats, such as deserts, are hot and dry, and others, such as the Arctic, are very cold. Other examples of habitats are mountains, oceans and savannahs. Animals need the right adaptations for each habitat. Adaptations are changes to an animal's body or the way it lives. These happen over a long time, and help an animal survive in its habitat.

Camel

Polar Bear

Elephant

Desert habitat
hot during the day, cold at night, very dry

Adaptations
1 doesn't need to drink or eat often
2 thick eyelashes
3 long legs
4 hump on its back
5 moves slowly

Why is this useful?
1 A
2
3
4
5

Arctic habitat
lots of ice, cold all year, short summers

Adaptations
1 small ears
2 long, strong legs
3 strong teeth and claws
4 very good sense of smell
5 thick, white fur

Why is this useful?
1 G
2
3
4
5

Savannah habitat
lots of grass, some trees, hot, not a lot of rain

Adaptations
1 no fur on its skin
2 large ears
3 long strong nose, or trunk
4 tusks
5 lives in family groups

Why is this useful?
1 E
2
3
4
5

3 Work in groups of three. The information from the 'Why is this useful?' columns is missing.
Find it in the list below and match it to the adaptations.

A ~~Water and food are hard to find in the desert.~~
B These keep the sand out of its eyes.
C With this, it can pick up water and reach leaves on trees.
D This has fat in it to use as food.
E ~~This helps it keep cool.~~
F These help it catch and kill prey.
G ~~These don't lose as much heat as big ears.~~
H These keep its body away from the hot sand.

I It uses these to dig for plants and to fight.
J They can learn from each other, and keep babies safe from predators like lions.
K These help it run fast and swim well.
L This helps it keep cool.
M It loses heat through these.
N This helps it find food.
O This keeps it warm and makes it difficult for other animals to see it.

4 Read the text and answer the questions.

1 Give two examples of different habitats. Describe those habitats.
2 Why do animals have adaptations?
3 Give three examples of different animal adaptations.
4 Why do camels move slowly?
5 Why do polar bears need strong legs?
6 Why do African elephants have large ears?

5 Complete the descriptions with *predator* or *prey*.

.............................: Other animals eat this animal.
.............................: This animal eats other animals.

6 Put these animals into the correct column of the table.

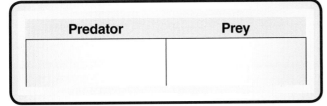

eagle
gazelle
zebra
cheetah
dolphin
lion
rabbit
mouse

7 Work with a partner. Write some sentences about three of the animals in Exercise 6. Think about their adaptations and why they are useful.

A mouse can run fast. This makes it difficult for predators to catch it.

Project Design an animal

Work in groups and design a new kind of animal.

• Choose a habitat for your animal.
• Is your animal a predator? Is it prey?
• Design your new animal. Think about
  – its body (eyes, ears, legs, fur, etc.)
  – how it lives (alone or in groups, when it sleeps, what it eats, etc.)
• Draw a picture of your animal and make notes about it. Give it a name.
• Tell the rest of the class all about your animal.

Predator	Prey

Review 5
Units 17-20

VOCABULARY

1 Each group of four words should make you think of another word.
Complete the word for each group.

0	aunt	cousin	brother	father	f <u>a</u> <u>m</u> <u>i</u> <u>l</u> y
1	mark	exam	term	teacher	s _ _ o _ _
2	dance	music	friends	fun	d _ _ _ o
3	pages	photos	articles	weekly	m _ _ _ z i _ e
4	play	actor	stage	seats	t _ _ a _ r _
5	job	instrument	play	person	m _ _ _ c _ _ n
6	win	enter	prize	talent show	c _ _ p _ _ _ _ _ _ n

2 Put the words in the right order to make questions.
Then complete the answers with an adverb of your choice.

1 can / dance / well / you / ?
No, I dance really ....

2 drive / your / does / fast / dad / ?
No, he drives quite ....

3 easily / you / new / do / things / learn / ?
No, I have to work very ....

4 always / you / school / speak / do / at / quietly / ?
No, sometimes I speak ....

3 Complete the sentences with the words in the box.

> album   cartoons   fan   notice   reviews   star

1 The film got good .... in the newspapers.
2 I love the Foo Fighters' first .... Their music's really good.
3 My little brother watches .... on TV when he gets home from school.
4 There's a .... in the school hall with information about the trip to the theatre.
5 My favourite film .... is Johnny Depp.
6 I'm a big .... of rock music. I love it!

GRAMMAR

4 Read the rules about entering the talent show.
Complete Emma's email to Leah with the words in the box.

> have to x3   don't have to   can   can't

Talent show

Rules for entering

Age: 14 or over

Groups: possible but only up to five people

Price to enter: £10 per person

Just fill in the form on our website!

Pay by July 31

To:	Leah
From:	Emma
Date:	May 2

I've got some information about the talent show. You **(1)** .... be 14 or over to enter. We **(2)** .... enter as a group but the group **(3)** .... have more than five people in it. If we want to enter, we **(4)** .... pay £10 each, and we **(5)** .... fill in a form on the website. We **(6)** .... pay yet, we can wait until the end of July. What do you think? Shall we do it?

5 ⊙ Choose the right word to complete the sentences.

1 He drives very *good* / *well.*
2 The weather there was very *good* / *well.*
3 *Shall* / *Can* you come to my house at 7 pm?

⊙ Correct the mistakes in these sentences.

4 Why not to see a film?
5 You don't bring anything except your clothes and your money.
6 I realy enjoyed it.
7 Lets play tennis at 4 pm.

LISTENING

6 ▶2.56 You'll hear a boy called Owen talking about a picture of his family. Listen and write the correct letter beside each name.

Lily	Nora	Abby	Colin ....
Rob	Liam	Grace	Max ....
Ryan		**Which person is Owen?**	

WRITING

7 Complete the email.

Write ONE word in each space.

Dear Samantha

I'm **(0)** .havíng. a great holiday here in Spain.
I've made **(1)** .... new friend. She's staying in
(2) .... same hotel. **(3)** .... name is
Natalya and she comes **(4)** .... Russia. She's a
year older **(5)** .... me.

Yesterday morning, we went **(6)** .... a bus to
visit a museum. There were lots **(7)** .... very
interesting things there. In the afternoon we climbed to
the top of the castle. **(8)** .... was very hot!

Please write and tell me **(9)** .... your holiday.

See **(10)** .... soon.

Love

Diana

SPEAKING

8 Put the words in the right order to make questions.

1 kind / programmes / TV / like / you / do / what /of / ?
2 subjects / favourite / at / what / are / your / school / ?
3 weekend / last / what / you / do / did / ?
4 you / often / go / how / to / do / cinema / the / ?
5 do / school / after / you / what / do / ?

Ask and answer the questions with your partner. Take turns to speak.

9 Now talk about your favourite film. Take turns to speak.

Tell me about your favourite film.

It's called …
It's about …
I like it because …

Get talking!

UNIT 2

EP Get talking!

Tell me about …
It's … . What about you?
Well, I …

1 ▶1.18 **Listen to Amber and Brad. What are they talking about?**

> family   friends   food   music   sport

2 Put Amber and Brad's sentences in the correct order and write the missing words.

I always have my racket in my bag! ☐

Well, I play .... ☐

Tell me about your favourite .... [1]

I practise on Mondays and Tuesdays and
  I play matches on Wednesdays. ☐

What about you? ☐

It's really fast and lots of fun. ☐

It's .... ☐

3 ▶1.19 **Listen and check.**

4 Choose a topic and write a conversation with your partner. Use the words in bold in Exercise 2.

> favourite food   clothes   your brother or sister

5 Read your conversation to another pair. Don't say the important words. They try to guess the topic. Take turns.

UNIT 4

EP Get talking!

I'm afraid … (not) …
Oh, that's a pity.
What a shame.

1 ▶1.31 **Listen to Kate, Jamie and Paul. Match the person to their problem.**

Kate   football
Jamie   concert
Paul   birthday party

2 Complete the conversations with the phrases in the box.

> I'm afraid I can't.   Oh, that's a pity.
> What a shame.

1 A: Can you come to my party on Saturday, Kate?
  K: What time?
  A: About three o'clock.
  K: .... I go swimming at three on Saturdays. Can I come later?
  A: Yes, of course! See you then.

2 A: Hi, Jamie, are you OK?
  J: No, not really. There's a football match this afternoon and I'm not in the team.
  A: .... Do you want to come cycling with me instead?
  J: Yeah, OK. Thanks.

3 A: Paul, I've got two tickets for the concert on Friday. Do you want to come with me?
  P: I'd love to but my dad says I can't go out this weekend. I've got exams next week.
  A: .... You can study on Saturday!
  P: I know! Tell my dad!

3 ▶1.31 **Listen again and check.**

4 Choose a conversation and practise with your partner. Remember, you're hearing bad news!

5 Choose your own topic and use the words from Exercise 2 to write your own conversation. Read your conversation to the class.

UNIT 6

1 ▶1.41 **Listen to the conversations. What are they about? Put the letters in the right order, then choose the right word.**

scimu   tsrop   okocgni

Conversation 1   ....
Conversation 2   ....
Conversation 3   ....

2 Which conversations are positive, and which are negative?

Conversation 1   ....
Conversation 2   ....
Conversation 3   ....

3 ▶1.42 **Listen to the conversations again. When you hear **, say the right words.**

1 A: How was the match?
   B: Terrible!
   A: Why?
   B: The game was really slow and there weren't any goals.
   A: **
   B: Yes. We played for 90 minutes. I was really tired.
   A: **

2 A: You're happy!
   B: I am! It was my violin exam yesterday.
   A: And?
   B: I passed! Now I can play in the school orchestra.
   A: **
   B: Thanks.

3 A: I've got a new job. I'm a cook!
   B: **
   A: Yeah. My friend knows I love cooking. I baked a birthday cake for his five-year-old sister. Now all my friends' parents want me to make cakes!
   B: **

4 Make a conversation with your partner. Use the positive or negative words.

UNIT 7

1 Read the sentences. Do you agree (✔) or disagree (✗)?

1 History is my favourite subject.

2 I love getting up early.

3 One Direction are a brilliant band.

2 ▶1.49 **Listen to Anna talking to her friends and answer the questions.**

Why doesn't …   Cristina like history?
              Peter like getting up early?
              Phil like One Direction?

3 ▶1.49 **Listen again and write their answers.**

Cristina: Hi, Anna. How was school today?
Anna: Hi, Cristina. It was a *great* day at school today. I have history on Tuesdays – it's my favourite subject.

Cristina: ....
The teacher always gives us lots of homework to do at the weekend.

Anna: I love getting up early because I can walk my dog before I go to school. Do you get up early, Peter?

Peter: ....
I like going to bed late and getting up late.

Anna: Hi, Phil. Did you see the One Direction concert on TV last night?
Phil: No, I can't stand One Direction.
Anna: But Phil, they're brilliant!
Phil: ....
I prefer rock music!

4 Write a sentence for each topic and tell your partner. Do you agree or disagree? If you disagree, say why. Use some of the sentences from the box at the top of the page.

Sport   School   Music   Food   Holiday

UNIT 10

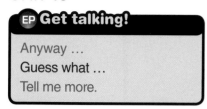

1 ▶1.68 **Listen to Louisa, Ian and Sophie. What are they talking about?**

> holidays   music   schools   shopping

2 ▶1.69 **Listen and check. Then answer the questions.**

1 What did Louisa do on Saturday?
2 Where did she go?
3 What did she do?
4 What was the problem?
5 What did she do?
6 What was the next problem?

3 **Read and complete the conversation below with the words in the box. Then practise with your partner.**

> Anyway   Guess what   Tell me more

A: Hi, *(name)*.

B: Hello, *(name)*.

A: (1) .... ? I saw the new Megan Fox film last night. It was great.

B: (2) .... ! I want to go to the cinema at the weekend.

A: Well, it was really fast and exciting, with these brilliant robots.

B: I can't stand films about robots. They're pretty boring, I think.

A: It was excellent. I love any films about robots! **(3)** .... , there are lots of other films to see this week.

UNIT 11

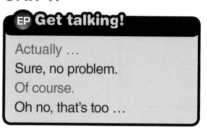

1 ▶2.05 **Listen and complete the conversation with the words in the box.**

A: OK, it's Emma's birthday next week and we need to plan her surprise party.

B: Right. My dad says we can have the party at our house.

A: Brilliant! How many people can we have?

B: My dad says no more than 15.

A: (1) .... , there are only ten of us, so that's perfect.

B: Good. We could start at around five o'clock?

A: (2) .... early. I think Emma plays basketball on Saturdays until five. How about six?

A: (3) .... Can you invite everyone?

B: (4) .... I can text them now.

2 **Read the conversation again and change the words in green to your own ideas.**

3 **Practise the new conversation with your partner.**

UNIT 13

EP Get talking!

That's a shame.
Oh dear.
Never mind.

1 ▶ 2.20 **Listen to Zac, Amy, Chris and Petra. They're talking to Daniel. Match the person to their problem.**

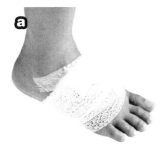

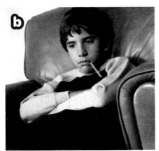

2 ▶ 2.20 **Look at the speech bubbles. Write what Daniel says. Listen again and check.**

I can't find my trainers.

(1) ....

I have only one hour to study.

(2) ....

I shouldn't play any more games this year.

(3) ....

The teacher wants to see everyone's projects today.

(4) ....

3 **Write three problems for your partner. Listen to your partner and say something to help. Take turns.**

A: I forgot to bring my lunch.
B: Never mind. You can share my lunch!

UNIT 15

EP Get talking!

Just a minute.
Right.
So …

1 **Put B's sentences in the right place to complete the conversation. There's one extra sentence that you don't need.**

a Nearly! I need my hat!
b Just a minute. Is it still snowing?
c So, Andrew … have you got my bag?
d Right. Got it! Let's go!
e OK, I'll get my gloves. Right. Got them.

A: Hurry up, the bus is coming!
B: (1) ....
A: Yes, it's really cold outside.
B: (2) ....
A: So … are you ready now?
B: (3) ....
A: Come on! The bus is here!
B: (4) ....
A: Just a minute. I need to use the bathroom!
B: [*sigh*]

2 ▶ 2.29 **Listen and check.**

3 ▶ 2.30 **Listen and repeat.**

4 **Now use the phrases in a conversation with a partner.**

Student A: Look at Units 1–6.
Student B: Look at Units 7–12.
Ask each other questions, like this. You must use the words in bold.
A: I've got some questions for you.
B: Right.
A: So, in Unit 1, what was … doing?
B: Just a minute, I'm thinking. … Was he/she ...?
You get one point for a correct answer.
You lose one point if you forget to use the words in bold.

UNIT 17

EP Get talking!

Would you like to …?
How about …?
I'd love to.

1 ▶2.40 **Listen to Ariana and Emily and answer the questions.**

1 When does Ariana want to go out?
2 What's the name of the TV programme?
3 How often is the TV programme on?
4 Where does Ariana want to meet Emily?

2 Look at the questions and choose the correct word.

1 Would you like *going* / *to go* to the cinema?
2 How about *going* / *to go* to the cinema?

3 Write a conversation. Use the questions to help you.

1 Where do you want to go?
2 Who do you want to go with?
3 What time do you want to meet?
4 Where do you want to meet?

4 Practise your conversation with your partner.

UNIT 18

EP Get talking!

Cool!
Sounds good.
You're right.
Good one!
Excellent idea.

1 ▶2.46 **Listen to some students talking about their ideas. Answer the questions. Sound positive!**

1 Hey, for our next holiday, how about going snowboarding in Canada?
2 Our teachers are really nice and work very hard. Let's make a big chocolate cake for them!
3 I haven't got any plans this weekend. Why don't we go to a concert?
4 I'm bored. There's nothing on television. Shall we watch a movie?
5 Robert Pattinson is my favourite actor. Why don't we go and see his new film?
6 I think we should have your party next month. A lot of people are on holiday this month.

2 ▶2.46 **Listen again. Now answer in a negative way. You can use the words in the box to help you.**

Oh no, that's boring.   Oh no, I hate …
No, I don't think so.   Sorry, I'm …

3 Write some ideas for your partner. You can use the words in the box to help you. Tell your partner what you think of their ideas.

How about   What about   Let's   Shall we
Why don't we   I think we should

Activities

UNIT 3 THIS IS THE MAD SCHOOL, EXERCISE 9

Student A

a) Your partner has information about a dance school. Ask your partner the questions from Exercise 8. Write the information in your notebook.

b) Here is some information about a music school. Use this information to answer your partner's questions.

The High Note School

School of classical music
For students from 15–19 years of age
Email: info4students@free.school
Mobile: 03 77 51 96 42

UNIT 10 BUYING AND SELLING ONLINE

Prepare to write

Chris: Well, I found a great jacket on the internet. It was black and it had a really cool design on the back. You can't pay in cash of course, so my mum paid for it with her credit card. After that, we waited and waited but it didn't come. After two weeks, I emailed the company but they didn't answer. Then, six days later, it finally arrived. But the jacket was the wrong size. It was too small *and* it was blue. I returned it and asked them to send me the right one but they emailed me to say they didn't have one in my size in black. And my mum is *still* waiting for them to return her money.

UNIT 3 THIS IS THE MAD SCHOOL, EXERCISE 9

Student B

a) Here is some information about a dance school. Use this information to answer your partner's questions.

b) Your partner has information about a music school. Ask your partner the questions from Exercise 8. Write the information in your notebook.

CULTURE: HOLLYWOOD

Read and check your ideas for Exercise 6.

1 The statuette is standing on a reel of film because people receive Oscars for their work in the films.
2 Each Oscar has a different number because the Academy need to have a record of who received each one.
3 The long sword has no meaning. It was part of the original design of the statuette.
4 There are different stories about why the statuette is called the 'Oscar'. One story is that a member of the Academy said that it looked like her uncle Oscar.
5 The Academy gives out about 50 Oscars each year.
6 An Oscar is very heavy!

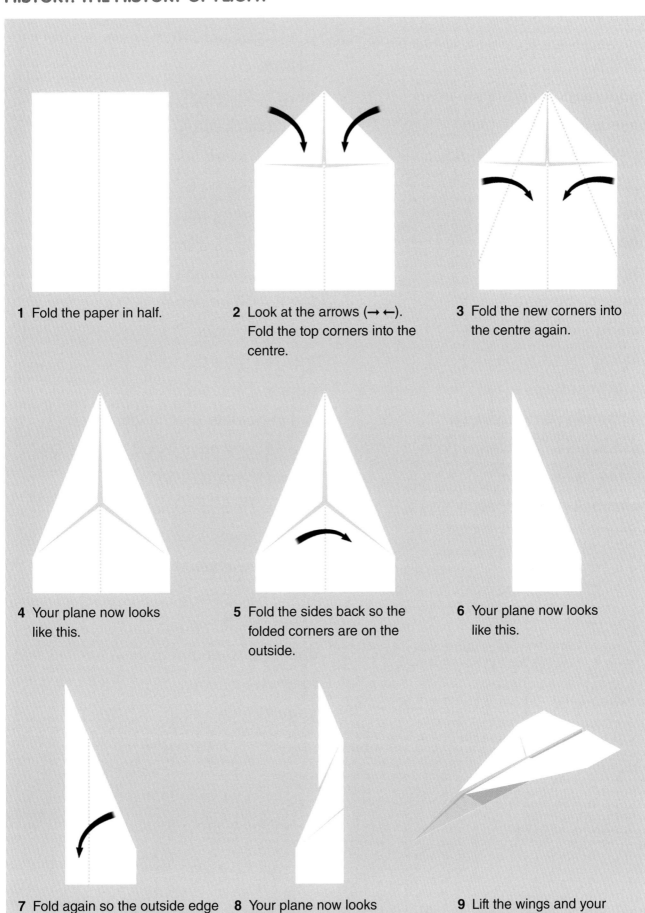

1 Fold the paper in half.

2 Look at the arrows (→ ←). Fold the top corners into the centre.

3 Fold the new corners into the centre again.

4 Your plane now looks like this.

5 Fold the sides back so the folded corners are on the outside.

6 Your plane now looks like this.

7 Fold again so the outside edge meets the centre fold line.

8 Your plane now looks like this.

9 Lift the wings and your plane is ready to fly.

EP Vocabulary list

UNIT 1

badminton /'bædmɪntən/ *noun*

baseball /'beɪsbɔːl/ *noun*

basketball /'bɑːskɪtbɔːl/ *noun*

cycling /'saɪklɪŋ/ *noun*

football /'fʊtbɔːl/ *noun*

hockey /'hɒki/ *noun*

rugby /'rʌgbi/ *noun*

running /'rʌnɪŋ/ *noun*

sailing /'seɪlɪŋ/ *noun*

skating /'skeɪtɪŋ/ *noun*

snowboarding /'snəʊbɔːdɪŋ/ *noun*

swimming /'swɪmɪŋ/ *noun*

table tennis /'teɪbl tenɪs/ *noun*

tennis /'tenɪs/ *noun*

volleyball /'vɒlibɔːl/ *noun*

UNIT 2

bowl /bəʊl/ *noun*

cabbage /'kæbɪdʒ/ *noun*

cereal /'sɪəriəl/ *noun*

chilli /'tʃɪli/ *noun*

cream /kriːm/ *noun*

cucumber /'kjuːkʌmbə/ *noun*

curry /'kʌri/ *noun*

fresh /freʃ/ *adjective*

fruit /fruːt/ *noun*

fruit tea /fruːt tiː/ *noun*

honey /'hʌni/ *noun*

hot chocolate /hɒt 'tʃɒklət/ *noun*

jam /dʒæm/ *noun*

lemon /'lemən/ *noun*

mango /'mæŋgəʊ/ *noun*

oil /ɔɪl/ *noun*

pan /pæn/ *noun*

rice /raɪs/ *noun*

salad /'sæləd/ *noun*

sauce /sɔːs/ *noun*

toast /təʊst/ *noun*

yogurt /'jɒgət/ *noun*

UNIT 3

actor /'æktə/ *noun*

album /'ælbəm/ *noun*

band /bænd/ *noun*

classical /'klæsɪkəl/ *adjective*

concert /'kɒnsət/ *noun*

drums /drʌmz/ *noun*

famous /'feɪməs/ *adjective*

jazz /dʒæz/ *noun*

keyboard /'kiːbɔːd/ *noun*

music /'mjuːzɪk/ *noun*

piano /piˈænəʊ/ *noun*

pop /pɒp/ *noun*

rap /ræp/ *noun*

record /rɪˈkɔːd/ *verb*

rock /rɒk/ *noun*

soul /səʊl/ *noun*

stage /steɪdʒ/ *noun*

violin /vaɪəˈlɪn/ *noun*

UNIT 4

big /bɪg/ *adjective*

broken /'brəʊkən/ *adjective*

date /deɪt/ *noun*

difficult /'dɪfɪkəlt/ *adjective*

expensive /ɪkˈspensɪv/ *adjective*

gold /gəʊld/ *noun*

old /əʊld/ *adjective*

plastic /'plæstɪk/ *noun*

round /raʊnd/ *adjective*

silver /'sɪlvə/ *noun*

square /skweə/ *adjective*

surprised /səˈpraɪzd/ *adjective*

wood /wʊd/ *noun*

writing /'raɪtɪŋ/ *noun*

EP Vocabulary list

UNIT 5

building /ˈbɪldɪŋ/ *noun*

climb /klaɪm/ *verb*

complete /kəmˈpliːt/ *verb*

cross /krɒs/ *verb*

crowded /ˈkraʊdɪd/ *adjective*

fire /faɪə/ *noun*

join /dʒɔɪn/ *verb*

open /ˈəʊpən/ *verb*

paint /peɪnt/ *verb*

person /ˈpɜːsən/ *noun*

play /pleɪ/ *verb*

rat /ræt/ *noun*

record /rɪˈkɔːd/ *verb*

sick /sɪk/ *adjective*

street /striːt/ *noun*

text /tekst/ *verb*

walk /wɔːk/ *verb*

wood /wʊd/ *noun*

UNIT 6

boss /bɒs/ *noun*

busy /ˈbɪzi/ *adjective*

customer /ˈkʌstəmə/ *noun*

earn /ɜːn/ *verb*

engineer /endʒɪˈnɪə/ *noun*

factory worker /ˈfæktəri wɜːkə/ *noun*

farmer /ˈfɑːmə/ *noun*

fisherman /ˈfɪʃəmən/ *noun*

football coach /ˈfʊtbɔːl kəʊtʃ/ *noun*

mechanic /məˈkænɪk/ *noun*

model /ˈmɒdəl/ *noun*

office /ˈɒfɪs/ *noun*

staff /stɑːf/ *noun*

weather man /ˈweðəmæn/ *noun*

UNIT 7

airport /ˈeəpɔːt/ *noun*

beach /biːtʃ/ *noun*

bike /baɪk/ *noun*

camping /ˈkæmpɪŋ/ *noun*

coach /kəʊtʃ/ *noun*

hotel /həʊˈtel/ *noun*

map /mæp/ *noun*

passport /ˈpɑːspɔːt/ *noun*

photo /ˈfəʊtəʊ/ *noun*

platform /ˈplætfɔːm/ *noun*

present /ˈprezənt/ *noun*

sightseeing /ˈsaɪtsiːɪŋ/ *noun*

swim /swɪm/ *verb*

take /teɪk/ *verb*

ticket /ˈtɪkɪt/ *noun*

train /treɪn/ *noun*

UNIT 8

armchair /ˈɑːmtʃeə/ *noun*

blanket /ˈblæŋkɪt/ *noun*

carpet /ˈkɑːpɪt/ *noun*

computer game /kəmˈpjuːtə geɪm/ *noun*

cupboard /ˈkʌbəd/ *noun*

diary /ˈdaɪəri/ *noun*

draw /drɔː/ *verb*

drawer /drɔː/ *noun*

drawing /ˈdrɔːɪŋ/ *noun*

drums /drʌmz/ *noun*

guitar /gɪˈtɑː/ *noun*

lamp /læmp/ *noun*

listen /ˈlɪsən/ *verb*

magazine /mægəˈziːn/ *noun*

music /ˈmjuːzɪk/ *noun*

paint /peɪnt/ *verb*

photograph /ˈfəʊtəgrɑːf/ *noun*

picture /ˈpɪktʃə/ *noun*

play /pleɪ/ *verb*

read /riːd/ *verb*

sea /siː/ *noun*

shelf /ʃelf/ *noun*

song /sɒŋ/ *noun*

sound /saʊnd/ *noun*

story /ˈstɔːri/ *noun*

wind /wɪnd/ *noun*

write /raɪt/ *verb*

EP Vocabulary list

UNIT 9

cap /kæp/ *noun*

cotton /ˈkɒtən/ *noun*

jacket /ˈdʒækɪt/ *noun*

jumper /ˈdʒʌmpə/ *noun*

leather /ˈleðə/ *noun*

plastic /ˈplæstɪk/ *noun*

shorts /ʃɔːts/ *noun*

socks /sɒks/ *noun*

swimming costume
   /ˈswɪmɪŋ kɒstjuːm/ *noun*

wool /wʊl/ *noun*

UNIT 10

earring /ˈɪərɪŋ/ *noun*

jewellery /ˈdʒuːəlri/ *noun*

leather /ˈleðə/ *noun*

make-up /ˈmeɪk ʌp/ *noun*

market /ˈmɑːkɪt/ *noun*

money /ˈmʌni/ *noun*

plastic /ˈplæstɪk/ *noun*

purse /pɜːs/ *noun*

sale /seɪl/ *noun*

shop /ʃɒp/ *noun*

sunglasses /ˈsʌnglɑːsɪz/ *noun*

wallet /ˈwɒlɪt/ *noun*

wool /wʊl/ *noun*

UNIT 11

burger /ˈbɜːgə/ *noun*

chicken leg /ˈtʃɪkɪn leg/ *noun*

cola /ˈkəʊlə/ *noun*

ice cream /aɪs kriːm/ *noun*

lemonade /leməˈneɪd/ *noun*

mineral water /ˈmɪnərəl wɔːtə/ *noun*

mushroom /ˈmʌʃruːm/ *noun*

pizza /ˈpiːtsə/ *noun*

salad /ˈsæləd/ *noun*

UNIT 12

clothes /kləʊðz/ *noun*

digital /ˈdɪdʒɪtəl/ *adjective*

download /daʊnˈləʊd/ *verb*

film /fɪlm/ *noun*

friend /frend/ *noun*

game /geɪm/ *noun*

homework /ˈhəʊmwɜːk/ *noun*

internet /ˈɪntənet/ *noun*

keyboard /ˈkiːbɔːd/ *noun*

laptop /ˈlæptɒp/ *noun*

machine /məˈʃiːn/ *noun*

memory /ˈmeməri/ *noun*

mouse /maʊs/ *noun*

music /ˈmjuːzɪk/ *noun*

picture /ˈpɪktʃə/ *noun*

printer /ˈprɪntə/ *noun*

screen /skriːn/ *noun*

speaker /ˈspiːkə/ *noun*

star /stɑː/ *noun*

tablet /ˈtæblət/ *noun*

video /ˈvɪdiəʊ/ *noun*

virus /ˈvaɪərəs/ *noun*

website /ˈwebsaɪt/ *noun*

EP Vocabulary list

UNIT 13

advice /əd'vaɪs/ *noun*

broken /'brəʊkən/ *adjective*

cold /kəʊld/ *noun*

enter /'entə/ *verb*

finish /'fɪnɪʃ/ *verb*

fit /fɪt/ *adjective*

headache /'hedeɪk/ *noun*

hurt /hɜːt/ *verb*

kilometres /'kɪləmiːtəz/ *noun*

pain /peɪn/ *noun*

race /reɪs/ *noun*

sick /sɪk/ *adjective*

stomach ache /'stʌmək eɪk/ *noun*

temperature /'temprətʃə/ *noun*

toothache /'tuːθeɪk/ *noun*

well /wel/ *adverb*

UNIT 14

bridge /brɪdʒ/ *noun*

building /'bɪldɪŋ/ *noun*

bus station /'bʌs steɪʃən/ *noun*

cycle tour /'saɪkl tʊə/ *noun*

park /pɑːk/ *noun*

petrol station /'petrəl steɪʃən/ *noun*

police station /pə'liːs steɪʃən/ *noun*

post office /'pəʊst ɒfɪs/ *noun*

river /'rɪvə/ *noun*

roundabout /'raʊndəbaʊt/ *noun*

sports centre /'spɔːts sentə/ *noun*

street /striːt/ *noun*

town centre /taʊn 'sentə/ *noun*

traffic light /'træfɪk laɪt/ *noun*

train station /'treɪn steɪʃən/ *noun*

walking tour /'wɔːkɪŋ tʊə/ *noun*

UNIT 15

cloudy /ˈklaʊdi/ *adjective*

dry /draɪ/ *adjective*

field /fiːld/ *noun*

foggy /ˈfɒgi/ *adjective*

footprint /ˈfʊtprɪnt/ *noun*

forest /ˈfɒrɪst/ *noun*

lake /leɪk/ *noun*

mountains /ˈmaʊntɪnz/ *noun*

sky /skaɪ/ *noun*

snow /snəʊ/ *noun*

snowy /ˈsnəʊi/ *adjective*

sunny /ˈsʌni/ *adjective*

thunderstorm /ˈθʌndəstɔːm/ *noun*

water /ˈwɔːtə/ *noun*

wet /wet/ *adjective*

windy /ˈwɪndi/ *adjective*

UNIT 16

bird /bɜːd/ *noun*

cat /kæt/ *noun*

dog /dɒg/ *noun*

elephant /ˈelɪfənt/ *noun*

horse /hɔːs/ *noun*

monkey /ˈmʌŋki/ *noun*

rabbit /ˈræbɪt/ *noun*

rat /ræt/ *noun*

sheep /ʃiːp/ *noun*

EP Vocabulary list

UNIT 17

cartoons /kɑːˈtuːnz/ *noun*

channel /ˈtʃænəl/ *noun*

competition /kɒmpəˈtɪʃən/ *noun*

excellent /ˈeksələnt/ *adjective*

fan /fæn/ *noun*

good-looking /ɡʊdˈlʊkɪŋ/ *adjective*

national /ˈnæʃənəl/ *adjective*

programme /ˈprəʊɡræm/ *noun*

record /rɪˈkɔːd/ *verb*

stage /steɪdʒ/ *noun*

star /stɑː/ *noun*

theatre /ˈθɪətə/ *noun*

TV /tiːˈviː/ *noun*

UNIT 18

advertisement /ədˈvɜːtɪsmənt/ *noun*

as /əz/ *conjunction*

because /bɪˈkəz/ *conjunction*

cartoon /kɑːˈtuːn/ *noun*

magazine /mæɡəˈziːn/ *noun*

newspaper /ˈnjuːzpeɪpə/ *noun*

notice /ˈnəʊtɪs/ *noun*

so /səʊ/ *conjunction*

when /wen/ *conjunction*

UNIT 19

activity /æk'tɪvɪti/ *noun*

art /ɑːt/ *noun*

Chinese /tʃaɪ'niːz/ *noun*

classroom /'klɑːsruːm/ *noun*

cost /kɒst/ *noun*

disco /'dɪskəʊ/ *noun*

film-making /'fɪlmmeɪkɪŋ/ *noun*

gym /dʒɪm/ *noun*

journey /'dʒɜːni/ *noun*

kitchen /'kɪtʃən/ *noun*

learn /lɜːn/ *verb*

lesson /'lesən/ *noun*

library /'laɪbrəri/ *noun*

maths /mæθs/ *noun*

music /'mjuːzɪk/ *noun*

nature /'neɪtʃə/ *noun*

pack /pæk/ *verb*

photography /fə'tɒgrəfi/ *noun*

project /'prɒdʒekt/ *noun*

repair /rɪ'peə/ *verb*

student /'stjuːdənt/ *noun*

study /'stʌdi/ *verb*

talk /tɔːk/ *verb*

teacher /'tiːtʃə/ *noun*

term /tɜːm/ *noun*

towel /taʊəl/ *noun*

uniform /'juːnɪfɔːm/ *noun*

video game /'vɪdiəʊ geɪm/ *noun*

watch /wɒtʃ/ *verb*

UNIT 20

almost /'ɔːlməʊst/ *adverb*

aunt /ɑːnt/ *noun*

brother /'brʌðə/ *noun*

child /tʃaɪld/ *noun*

children /'tʃɪldrən/ *noun*

cousin /'kʌzən/ *noun*

daughter /'dɔːtə/ *noun*

especially /ɪ'speʃəli/ *adverb*

father /'fɑːðə/ *noun*

grandchild /'græntʃaɪld/ *noun*

granddaughter /'grændɔːtə/ *noun*

grandfather /'grænfɑːðə/ *noun*

grandmother /'grænmʌðə/ *noun*

grandparent /'grænpeərənt/ *noun*

grandson /'grænsʌn/ *noun*

mother /'mʌðə/ *noun*

nearly /'nɪəli/ *adverb*

quite /kwaɪt/ *adverb*

really /'rɪəli/ *adverb*

sister /'sɪstə/ *noun*

son /sʌn/ *noun*

uncle /'ʌŋkl/ *noun*

Grammar reference

STARTER UNIT

BE

Positive	Negative
I'm (am) you/we/they're (are) he/she/it's (is)	I'm (am) not you/we/they aren't (are not) he/she/it isn't (is not)
Questions	**Short answers**
Am I ...? Are you/we/they ...? Is he/she/it ...?	Yes, I am. No, I'm not. Yes, you/we/they are. No, you/we/they aren't. Yes, he/she/it is. No, he/she/it isn't.

- We use *be* for people and things to describe them, say how old they are, where they are, etc.
  I'm John. I'm tall. I'm 14. I'm in the classroom.
  My bag is under my desk. It's blue and white.

THERE IS / THERE ARE

	Singular	Plural
Positive	there's	there are
Negative	there isn't	there aren't
Questions	Is there ...?	Are there ...?
Short answers	Yes, there is. No, there isn't.	Yes, there are. No, there aren't.

- We use *there is / there are* to say that something exists (or doesn't exist).
  ***There's** a rubber in my pencil case but **there aren't** any pencils.*
- We use *there is* with singular and uncountable nouns.
  *'**Is there** a window near your desk?'*
  *'Yes, **there is**.'*
- We use *there are* with plural countable nouns.
  *'**Are there** any pens on the table?' 'Yes, **there are**.'*

Practice

1 Complete the questions with *Is there* or *Are there*. Then write the answer.

    0 *Are there* any shelves in your classroom?
       (✔) *Yes, there are.*
    1 .... a green pencil on the floor?
       (✔) ....
    2 .... any maps on the walls?
       (✘) ....
    3 .... any cinemas in your town?
       (✔) ....

HAVE GOT

Positive
I/you/we/they've (have) got he/she/it's (has) got
Negative
I/you/we/they haven't (have not) got he/she/it hasn't (has not) got
Questions
Have I/you/we/they got ...? Has he/she/it got ...?
Short answers
Yes, I/you/we/they have.   No, you/we/they haven't. Yes, he/she/it has.   No, he/she/it hasn't.

- We use *have got* to talk about our family, our hair or eyes and our possessions.
  I've got a brother. He's got blue eyes.
  My sister's got a new phone. It's great!

Practice

2 Complete the sentences with the correct form of *have got*.

    0 ...*I've got*... a new green bike.
    1 My friends .... (✘) pets at home.
    2 We .... a new English teacher.
    3 My dad .... (✘) a car. He .... a bike.
    4 '............ you .... a computer?' 'Yes, I ....'

CAN

Positive
I/you/he/she/it/we/they can
Negative
I/you/he/she/it/we/they can't (cannot)
Questions
Can I/you/he/she/it/we/they ...?
Short answers
Yes, I/you/he/she/it/we/they can. No, I/you/he/she/it/we/they can't.

- We use *can* to talk about ability.
  I can play football but I can't play tennis.

Practice

3 Write four sentences about the things you can and you can't do.

    I can't speak French but I can speak English.

UNIT 1

ADVERBS OF FREQUENCY

Present simple

Positive	I/You/We/They **play** volleyball. He/She/It **goes** running.
Negative	I/You/We/They **don't play** hockey. He/She/It **doesn't go** cycling.
Questions	Do I/you/we/they **play** rugby? Does he/she/it **go** sailing?
Short answers	Yes, I/you/we/they **do**. No, I/you/we/they **don't**. Yes, he/she/it **does**. No, he/she/it **doesn't**.

We use the **present simple** to talk about things we do often or every day.

I **play** football after school every day.

He **doesn't go** skating in the winter.

Adverbs of frequency

- 100%   I *always* play tennis in the summer.
  I *usually* go running with my dad.
  I *often* play football with my friends.
  I'm *sometimes* late for school.
  0%   I'm *never* unhappy.

- We use the present simple with **adverbs of frequency** to say how often we do things.
  How **often** do you go snowboarding?
  We **sometimes** go snowboarding in the winter.

- With the verb *be*, we put the adverb after the verb and before the adjective.
  Are you **sometimes tired** after school?
  Yes, I'm **often tired**. / No I'm not **often tired**.

- With other verbs in the present simple, we put the adverb before the main verb.
  Do you **often play** hockey at school?
  Yes, I **often play** hockey. / No, I **don't often play** hockey.

- Remember that with **never**, we don't use the verb in the negative.
  I **never go** snowboarding. (**not** ~~I don't never go...~~)

Practice

1 Complete the sentences with the present simple form of the verbs in the box.

> play   watch   not go
> study   not play   go

1 I .... basketball in a team.
2 My teacher .... sailing when the weather is bad.
3 My brother .... TV after dinner every day.
4 .... your mum .... running before work?
5 My friends and I .... rugby at the weekend. We prefer football.
6 My best friend always .... hard before an exam.

2 Rewrite the sentences with the adverb of frequency in brackets in the correct place.

0 I'm late for school. (always)
   I'm always late for school.
1 We play badminton. (never)
   ....
2 My dad doesn't go running. (often)
   ....
3 My friends and I go cycling. (sometimes)
   ....
4 We aren't bored in our sports lesson. (usually)
   ....
5 Are you tired in the morning? (often)
   ....

3 Put the words in order to make questions. Then write true answers for you.

0 play / you / tennis / how often / do / ?
   How often do you play tennis?
   I sometimes play tennis.
1 you and your friends / go / often / sailing / do / ?
   ....
   ....
2 you / sometimes / bored / are / at home / ?
   ....
   ....
3 dinner / how often / cook / you / do / ?
   ....
   ....
4 your best friend / how often / watch / does / TV / ?
   ....
   ....
5 sometimes / do / you / go / alone / running / ?
   ....
   ....

UNIT 2

PRESENT CONTINUOUS AND PRESENT SIMPLE

→ **See** Grammar reference, **Unit 1, Present simple p.143**

Present continuous

Positive	I'm (am) **making** pancakes. You/We/They**'re (are) mixing** eggs and milk. He/She/It**'s (is) adding** the sugar.
Negative	I'm (am) **not making** lunch. You/We/They **aren't (are not) cooking**. (*or* You/We/They**'re not cooking**.) He/She/It **isn't (is not) helping**. (*or* He/She/It**'s not helping**.)
Questions	**Am** I **eating** pancakes? **Are** you/we/they **making** breakfast? **Is** he/she/it **drinking** hot chocolate?
Short answers	Yes, I **am**. No, I'm **not**. Yes, you/we/they **are**. No, you/we/they **aren't**. (*or* you/we/they**'re not**.) Yes, he/she/it **is**. No, he/she/it **isn't**. (*or* he/she/it**'s not**.)

Spelling: *-ing* form

most verbs add *-ing*	*cook → cooking* *mix → mixing* *add → adding*
verbs ending in *-e*: remove *-e* and add *-ing*	*make → making* *have → having*
verbs ending in *-ie*: change the *-ie* to *-y* and add *-ing*	*lie → lying*
one-syllable verbs ending in a consonant + a vowel + a consonant (except *w*, *x* or *y*): double the consonant and add *-ing*	*get up → getting up* *shop → shopping*
two-syllable verbs ending in a stressed vowel + a consonant: double the consonant and add *-ing*	*begin → beginning* (**but** *open → opening*)
In British English, we double the final *l* in *travel*.	*travel → travelling* (American English: *travel → traveling*)

We use:

• the **present simple** to talk about things we do often or every day. We often use it with frequency adverbs like **often, usually, never**, etc.
*We **often eat** salad in the summer.*

• the **present continuous** to talk about things we're doing now or at the moment. We often use it with words like **now, at the moment, today**, etc.
*I'm **making** pancakes **at the moment**.*

Practice

1 **Write complete sentences in the present continuous.**

   0 My brother / make chocolate sauce at the moment.
     My brother's making chocolate sauce at the moment.

   1 We / serve dinner now.

   2 I / not swim today.

   3 What / you make?

   4 My friends / not go cycling at the moment.

   5 your best friend / sit next to you?

2 **Circle the correct words to complete the sentences.**

   1 We *never eat* / *'re never eating* curry and rice.

   2 I *go* / *'m going* swimming after school every day.

   3 Shh! The baby *sleeps* / *'s sleeping* at the moment.

   4 What *do you usually have* / *are you usually having* for breakfast?

   5 What *do you watch* / *are you watching* on TV now?

   6 My mum *doesn't work* / *isn't working* today. She's on holiday.

3 **Complete the sentences so they are true for you.**

   1 For breakfast, I often ....

   2 My friends and I sometimes .... after school.

   3 At the moment, my best friend ....

   4 I'm wearing .... today.

   5 On Friday afternoon, I usually ....

   6 I .... now.

UNIT 3

LIKE, DON'T LIKE, HATE, LOVE + -ING

After **like**, **don't like**, **hate** and **love**, we use the **-ing** form.

*My sister **loves listening** to rap.*

- ☺ *I really love playing the drums.*
  I love listening to the piano.
  I like listening to rock music.
  I quite like playing the guitar.
  ☹ *I don't like listening to jazz.*
  I hate listening to the violin.

- We use **like**, **don't like**, **hate** and **love** to talk about the things we like or don't like doing.
  *I **love playing** the piano.*
  *My friends **don't like going** to concerts.*

- We can use **really** to say how much we like, love or hate doing things.
  We also can use **quite** with **like**.
  *I **really love** listening to music but I **really hate** listening to rap.*
  *I **quite like** playing the keyboards. (**not** I quite love or I quite hate)*

  → **See Grammar reference, Unit 2, Spelling: *-ing* form, p.144**

Practice

1 Write the *-ing* form of the verbs in the box in the correct columns.

> ~~dance~~   get up   have   make   open   play   shop   sit   swim   watch

write → writing	run → running	help → helping	listen → listening
dancing			

2 Complete the sentences with the *-ing* form of the verbs in brackets.

1 My sister really loves .... (play) the guitar.
2 My grandparents like .... (live) in a big city.
3 My dad loves .... (drive).
4 I quite like .... (go) snowboarding with my family.
5 My friends and I hate .... (wear) a school uniform.
6 We don't like .... (get up) early.

3 Write true sentences for you with *like, don't like, hate, love* and the words in brackets.

1 (go cycling) I really love going cycling with my friends .
2 (listen to rock music) ....
3 (study for exams) ....
4 (have pizza) ....
5 (swim in the sea) ....
6 (dance) ....

UNIT 4

WAS/WERE: +, −, ?

Positive	I/He/She/It **was** at home yesterday. You/We/They **were** at school at ten o'clock.
Negative	I/He/She/It **wasn't** (**was not**) five years old in 2000. You/We/They **weren't** in the lake yesterday.
Questions	Where **was** I/he/she/it at six o'clock? Who **were** you/we/they with yesterday? **Was** I/he/she/it late? **Were** you/we/they happy?
Short answers	Yes, I/he/she/it **was**. No, I/he/she/it **wasn't** (**was not**). Yes, you/we/they **were**. No, you/we/they weren't (**were not**).

Was/were are the past forms of *be*. We use *was/were* to describe people and things in the past.

*My grandmother **was** tall and she was very beautiful.*

*The earrings **were** silver. They **were** round.*

We also use *was/were* to say where people or things were in the past.

*We **weren't** at school yesterday. It was a holiday.*

*The ring **wasn't** in her bedroom.*

Practice

1 Complete these sentences with *was(n't)* or *were(n't)*.

0 I ..*was*.. very surprised.
1 My friends .... interested in my new ring.
2 My dad .... (not) in the office at 11 o'clock.
3 We .... (not) happy. Our dog .... missing.
4 You .... very tired yesterday.
5 I .... (not) hungry but I .... very thirsty.

2 Put these words in order to make questions. Then write the short answer.

0 bored / you / were / ? (✔)
    'Were you bored?' 'Yes, I was.'
1 your / tall / teacher / was / first / ? (✔)

2 shoes / were / his / broken / ? (✔)

3 you / and / friends / your / cold / were / ? (✘)

4 mobile / bag / was / in / your / your / ? (✘)

5 lake / were / the / we / near / ? (✔)

3 Write complete questions with *was* or *were*. Then write true answers for you.

0 Where / you / yesterday / at 6 pm?
    Where were you yesterday at 6 pm?
    I was at home.
1 you / late / for school on Monday?

2 your friends / tired / at 9 am this morning?

3 When / your best friend / born?

4 What day / it / yesterday?

5 this exercise / difficult?

UNIT 5

PAST SIMPLE: REGULAR VERBS

> I/You/He/She/It/We/They **climbed** a mountain.
> I/You/He/She/It/We/They **recorded** an album.

- We use the past simple to talk about things that happened in the past.
  Leonardo da Vinci **painted** *the* Mona Lisa.
  Aristide Boucicaut **opened** *the first department store in Paris.*
- With regular verbs, the past simple verb ends in *-ed*. (See Spelling below.)
  *climb → climb**ed**, change → chang**ed**,*
  *carry → carr**ied***

Spelling: regular verbs

most verbs: add *-ed*	*play → play**ed***
verbs that end in *-e*: add *-d*	*change → chang**ed***
verbs that end in consonant + *-y*: change *-y* to *-i* and add *-ed*	*carry → carr**ied***
one-syllable verbs ending in a consonant + a vowel + a consonant (except *w*, *x* or *y*): double the consonant and add *-ed*	*stop → sto**pped***
two-syllable verbs ending in a stressed vowel + a consonant: double the final consonant and add *-ed*	*prefer → prefe**rred***
In British English, we double the final *l*.	*travel → trave**lled*** (American English: *travel → trave**led***)

Practice

1 Complete the columns with the past simple form of the verbs in the box.

> cross   die   enjoy   plan   practise
> shop   stay   study   try   walk

climb → climbed	change → changed	carry → carried	play → played	stop → stopped
			crossed	

2 Complete the sentences with the past simple form of the verbs in the box.

> climb   finish   listen
> play   try   watch

1 My friends .... football yesterday.
2 I .... TV last night.
3 We .... to music in class.
4 My mum .... a mountain at the weekend.
5 My family .... Chinese food last week.
6 I .... my homework quickly.

Past simple with *in* and *on*

- We often use *in* and *on* with the past simple to say when things happened.
- We use *on* for the date and the day.
  We cooked pancakes **on** *17th February /* **on** *5th April 2005 /* **on** *Tuesday, etc.*
- We use *in* for months, years and centuries.
  She recorded her first album **in** *May /* **in** *2008 /* **in** *October 1999 /* **in** *the 20th century, etc.*

Practice

3 Write complete sentences in the past simple with *in* or *on*.

0 Neil Armstrong / walk / on the moon / 21st July 1969
  Neil Armstrong walked on the moon on 21st July 1969.

1 I / cook / dinner / Tuesday
  ....
  ....

2 We / study / Leonardo da Vinci / 2011
  ....
  ....

3 My dad / work / in New York / May
  ....
  ....

4 My uncle / stop / playing football / September 1997
  ....
  ....

5 My cousins / stay / in an expensive hotel / 3rd March
  ....
  ....

UNIT 6

PAST SIMPLE: ?, –

→ See Grammar reference, Unit 5, Past simple of regular verbs, p.147

Negative
I/You/He/She/It/We/They **didn't (did not) finish**.
Questions
Where **did** I/you/he/she/it/we/they **cook**?
Did I/you/he/she/it/we/they work in a shop?
Short answers
Yes, I/you/he/she/it/we/they **did**.
No, I/you/he/she/it/we/they **didn't**.

* We use the **past simple negative** to talk about things that didn't happen in the past.

  *The café **didn't open** at eight o'clock.*
  *We **didn't watch** a film in class.*

* We use **past simple questions** to ask about things that happened in the past.

  *What time **did** he **finish** work?*
  *'**Did** you **listen** to music last night?' 'Yes, I **did**.'*

Practice

1 Complete the sentences with the past simple negative form of the verbs in blue.

   0 My dad played tennis. He .....*didn't play*.... volleyball.

   1 We cooked fish. We .... meat.

   2 In the school holidays, my brother worked in a factory. He .... in a shop.

   3 I used my mobile to send a message. I .... the computer.

   4 My friends climbed a tree. They .... a mountain.

   5 I opened the window. I .... the door.

2 Use the past simple negative and the words in brackets to write true sentences about what you and the people you know didn't do yesterday.

   0 (I / watch)
   ....*I didn't watch a film on TV yesterday.*....

   1 (my mum / listen)

   ....

   2 (my classmates / walk)

   ....

   3 (I / study)

   ....

   4 (my friends and I / play)

   ....

   5 (this class / start)

   ....

3 Write complete questions in the past simple. Then write the short answers.

   0 ..*Did*.. you ..*cook*.. (cook) dinner yesterday?
   No, ..*I didn't*....

   1 .... your sister .... (help) you with your homework?
   Yes, ...

   2 .... your friends .... (finish) all the biscuits?
   Yes, ...

   3 .... this class .... (start) at 10 am?
   No, ...

   4 .... you .... (enjoy) the party?
   Yes, ...

   5 .... it .... (rain) yesterday?
   No, ...

4 Put the words in order to make questions. Then write true answers for you.

   0 you / walk / this / did / school / to / morning / ?
   ..*Did you walk to school this morning?*....
   ..*Yes, I did.*..

   1 start / what / you / did / time / school / ?

   ....
   ....

   2 use / did / a / you / computer / last night / ?

   ....
   ....

   3 study / yesterday / you / did / what / ?

   ....
   ....

   4 visit / country / holiday / you / did / another / on / ?

   ....
   ....

   5 when / you / finish / Unit 5 / did / ?

   ....
   ....

UNIT 7

PAST SIMPLE: IRREGULAR VERBS

→ See Grammar reference, **Unit 5**, Past simple of regular verbs, p.147

→ See Grammar reference, **Unit 6**, Past simple: questions and negatives, p.148

Positive	I/You/He/She/It/We/They **swam** in the sea every day.
Negative	I/You/He/She/It/We/They **didn't go** to Italy on holiday.
Questions	What **did** I/you/he/she/it/we/they **eat**? **Did** I/you/he/she/it/we/they **have** a good time?
Short answers	Yes, I/you/he/she/it/we/they **did**. No, I/you/he/she/it/we/they **didn't**.

- Remember, we use the **past simple** to talk about things that happened or didn't happen in the past.
- With regular verbs, the past simple verb ends in **-ed**.
  want → want**ed**, decide → decid**ed**, travel → travel**led**
- With irregular verbs, the past simple doesn't end in **-ed**. (See irregular verb list p.163.)
  buy → **bought**, come → **came**, take → **took**

Practice

1 Complete the table.

Verb	Past simple	Verb	Past simple
eat	**(0)** ate	arrive	**(6)** ....
(1)	went	**(7)**	carried
ride	**(2)**	enjoy	**(8)** ....
(3)	saw	**(9)**	lived
swim	**(4)**	stop	**(10)** ....
(5)	took	**(11)**	watched

2 Read the sentences and <u>underline</u> the irregular past simple form. Then write the infinitive.

0 I <u>swam</u> in the sea every day. ..swim..
1 We went sightseeing in the morning. ....
2 We had a great time on holiday. ....
3 I rode an elephant in India. ....
4 My friends ate pizza last night. ....
5 My parents bought me a present. ....

3 Complete the sentences with the past simple form of the verbs in the box.

buy	can	get up
give	ride	see

1 Our teacher .... us a lot of homework.
2 We .... our bikes to the beach.
3 I .... some trainers in the new department store.
4 My dad .... at six o'clock this morning.
5 I .... my best friend with her mum.
6 I .... read and write when I was five.

4 Use the past simple form of the verbs in brackets to complete the conversation.

Alice: How **(0)** ..was.. (be) your holiday?

Neil: Great! I really **(1)** .... (enjoy) it!

Alice: **(2)** .... you .... (go) camping?

Neil: No, we **(3)** .... (stay) in a hotel.

Alice: What **(4)** .... you .... (do) every day?

Neil: In the morning, we **(5)** .... (swim) in the sea. The beach **(6)** .... (be) very near. In the afternoon, we **(7)** .... (visit) different places.

Alice: Cool! Where **(8)** .... you .... (eat)?

Neil: We **(9)** .... (have) breakfast and dinner in the hotel. I **(10)** .... (take) a lot of photos.

Alice: Can I see them?

Neil: Yes, of course.

UNIT 8

SOMEONE, ANYONE, ETC.

	some-	any-	no-
Person	someone	anyone	no one
Thing	something	anything	nothing
Place	somewhere	anywhere	nowhere

- We normally use **someone, something**, etc. in positive sentences and **anyone, anything**, etc. in negative sentences and questions.

  There's **something** to drink on the table.

  I haven't got **anywhere** to sit.

  Is there **anyone** in the classroom?

- **No one, nothing**, etc. mean *not anyone, not anything*, etc. so we don't use a negative verb with these words.

  I've got **nothing** to drink. (not ~~I haven't got nothing~~ ...)

  There's **nowhere** to sit. (not ~~There isn't nowhere~~ ...)

Practice

1 Circle the correct words to complete the sentences.

1 I'm bored. I haven't got *anyone / anything / anywhere* to do.

2 I went to the new department store but I bought *no one / nothing / nowhere*.

3 There's a skate park near here. Is there *anyone / anything / anywhere* to skate in your town?

4 Are you busy? I'm looking for *someone / something / somewhere* to help me with my homework.

5 Where are your friends? There's *no one / nothing / nowhere* in the classroom.

6 They decided to go *someone / something / somewhere* near a beach for their holiday.

2 Complete the sentences with some-, any- or no-.

0 Your room's very tidy. There's ...no..thing on the floor.

1 I'm leaving because there isn't ....where for me to sit.

2 There isn't ....one in my class who speaks German.

3 I saw ....one famous at the cinema but I don't know his name.

4 Was there ....thing good on TV last night?

5 My favourite place is ....where I can play football with my friends.

3 Complete the conversations with the words in the box.

anything	anywhere	no one
nothing	someone	~~something~~
somewhere		

0 **A:** Are you hungry?
  B: No, I ate ..*something*.. a few minutes ago.

1 **A:** What's that noise? I think there's .... outside the window.
  B: No, it's the trees. There's .... there.

2 **A:** Did you go .... special yesterday?
  B: Yes, we went .... near the lake and we had a picnic.

3 **A:** Are you doing ...., Jack?
  B: No, ... Why?

UNIT 9

PRONOUNS AND DETERMINERS

	Determiner	Pronoun
I	It's my jumper.	It's mine.
you	It's your cap.	It's yours.
he	It's his jacket.	It's his.
she	It's her swimming costume	It's hers.
it	It's its shoe.	–
we	They're our clothes.	They're ours.
you	They're your socks.	They're yours.
they	They're their trousers.	They're theirs.

- We use the determiners **my, your, his**, etc. with nouns to talk about our possessions.
  *That's **my** pencil case.*
  *Is this **your** cap?*
- We use the pronouns **mine, yours, his**, etc. so we don't need to repeat the noun.
  *'Is this your cap?' 'Yes, it's **mine**.'* (**not** ~~Yes, it's my cap.~~)
  *'Are these your shoes?' 'Yes, they're **ours**.'* (**not** ~~Yes, they're our shoes.~~)
- **Mine** is always singular.
  *'Who do these shoes belong to?' 'They're **mine**.'*
  (**not** ~~mines~~)
- There is no pronoun form for **its**.

Practice

1 Complete the sentences with the correct determiner (*my, your, his*, etc.).

1 I love watching films. .... favourite actor is Johnny Depp.

2 One of my uncles lives in New York. .... name is David.

3 That isn't my parents' car. .... car is blue.

4 'Is this Maria's?' 'No, ... jacket is red.'

5 We haven't got a big dog. .... dog is quite small.

6 Can I borrow .... rubber, please? I haven't got one.

2 Circle the correct words.

1 You haven't got John's cap. *His / Hers* is black.

2 I haven't got a pencil. Can I borrow *mine / yours*?

3 These books belong to Harry and Nick. Where are *ours / hers*?

4 Ana's looking for her shoes. Are these *hers / theirs*?

5 You're wearing Nick's jumper. Where's *his / yours*?

6 Shall we buy a new tent? *Ours / Its* is very old.

3 Complete the conversation with the words in the box.

> his   mine   my   our
> theirs   your   yours   yours

Steve: We did the washing yesterday. I think **(1)** .... clothes are dry now. Are these shorts **(2)** ....?

Laura: No, they aren't. They're Dan's.

Steve: And these green socks? Are they **(3)** .... too?

Laura: No, they're **(4)** .... The white socks are Dan's.

Steve: Right. I like **(5)** .... socks, Laura!

Laura: **(6)** .... grandma gave them to me!

Steve: Whose blue jumper is this?

Laura: It's **(7)** ....! You've got a blue jumper, haven't you!

Steve: You're right! Dan and Lucy have got red caps. Are these **(8)** ....?

Laura: Yes, they are.

UNIT 10

SOME, ANY, A BIT OF, A FEW, A LOT OF

	Countable	Uncountable
Questions	Are there **any shops** near your house?	Have you got **any money**?
Positive	There are **some shops** over there.	There's **some money** on the table.
Negative	There aren't **any** large **shops** near my house.	I haven't got **any money** in my purse.
a lot of	My sister's got **a lot of earrings**.	My mum's got **a lot of jewellery**.
a few / a bit of	There are **a few books** on the table.	There's **a bit of make-up** in the bathroom.

- Countable nouns are nouns that we can count. We can use *a/an*, *the* or a number before them and they can be used in both the singular and the plural.

  *I bought **a new wallet, two caps** and **a book** in the department store.*

- Uncountable nouns are nouns that we can't count. We can't use *a/an* or a number before them and we can't use them in the plural.

  *My cousin bought **some jewellery** and **some make-up**.* (**not** *a jewellery, a make-up*)

Practice

1 Complete the table with the words in the box.

> biscuit   cheese   cola   earring   egg
> jacket   jewellery   make-up   milk   money
> photo   purse   T-shirt   wallet

Countable	Uncountable
biscuit	cheese

2 Complete the sentences with *some* or *any*.

1 I didn't buy a new wallet because I didn't have .... money.

2 There are .... new students in my class.

3 Were there .... blue T-shirts in the shop?

4 Let's go shopping. I want to buy .... new clothes.

5 That shop hasn't got .... bread.

6 Did you eat .... cake on your birthday?

3 Complete the sentences with *a lot of*, *a few* or *a bit of*.

0 Sally's got ...*a bit of*... jewellery but not much.

1 We've got .... biscuits. There are three packets here and four packets on that shelf.

2 We did well in our test so our teacher only gave us .... homework – just one exercise.

3 I've got .... good friends – Anna, Karen and Rachel.

4 We made sandwiches, pizza, burgers and chicken legs. There was .... food at my party!

5 The trip is for three days. You only need .... pairs of socks, not 12 pairs!

4 Circle the correct words to complete the conversation.

James: Did you buy **(1)** *a / any* clothes in the sales?

Holly: Yes, I bought **(2)** *any / some* sunglasses, **(3)** *a / some* baseball cap and **(4)** *a few / a bit of* make-up.

James: Really! You bought a **(5)** *lot / few* of things. I only bought **(6)** *a / some* wallet.

UNIT 11

AS ... AS

When we compare two things:

- we can use **as** + **adjective** + **as** to say the things are the same.

  *In my school, pizza is **as popular as** burgers.*
  (**not** ~~as popular than~~ ...)

- we use **not as** + **adjective** + **as** to say two things are different.

  *Chocolate cake is**n't as healthy as** fruit salad.*
  The form of the adjective doesn't change when we use **as** + **adjective** + **as**.
  *A burger is**n't as big** as a pizza.* (**not** ~~as bigger as~~ ...)

Practice

1 Complete the sentences with as ... as.

- **0** I'm short but my sister is very short.
  I'm not ..*as short as my sister*.............. .

- **1** The Burger Bar is popular. The Pizza Restaurant is popular too.
  The Burger Bar is ....
  ....

- **2** Ireland is wet. Scotland is wet too.
  Ireland is ....
  ....

- **3** Lemonade is sweet but cola is really sweet.
  Lemonade isn't ....
  ....

- **4** Your shorts are quite dirty but your T-shirt is very dirty.
  Your shorts aren't ....
  ....

- **5** My mum's pizza is good. The pizza at Harry's Café is good too.
  My mum's pizza is ....
  ....

COMPARATIVE ADJECTIVES

Adjective	Comparative
one syllable	
slow →	slower
two syllables with consonant + -y	
healthy →	healthier
two syllables or more	
beautiful →	more beautiful
irregular	
good →	better
bad →	worse
far →	farther/further

- We use comparative adjectives to compare two things (see Spelling).

  *Water is usually **cheaper** than cola.*

- We usually use **than** after comparative adjectives.

  *Vegetables are **healthier than** biscuits.*

Spelling

One-syllable adjectives:

- mostly add -er.
  *small → small**er**, cheap → cheap**er***

- if they end in -e, add -r.
  *nice → nice**r**, late → late**r***

- if they end in consonant + vowel + consonant (except w, x or y), double the consonant and add -er.
  *big → bi**gg**er, fat → fa**tt**er*

Two-syllable adjectives ending in consonant + -y change the -y to -i and add -er.
*busy → bus**ier**, happy → happ**ier***

Two or more syllables add **more**.
*expensive → **more** expensive*

Practice

2 Complete the sentences with the comparative form of the adjective.

- **1** My maths teacher is .... (young) than my geography teacher.
- **2** I think playing football is .... (interesting) than watching it.
- **3** Exercise 2 is .... (easy) than Exercise 3.
- **4** My house is .... (far) from school than yours.
- **5** A blue whale is .... (big) than an elephant.

3 Write complete sentences. Use the comparative form of the adjectives in the box.

~~expensive~~ fast good hot

- **0** The blue T-shirt is £10. The red T-shirt £15.
  The red T-shirt is ..*more expensive than the blue T-shirt*............... .
- **1** It's 2 hours by train. It's 2 hours 45 minutes by bus.
  The train is ....
  ....
- **2** It's 25°C in London today. It's 33°C in Istanbul.
  Istanbul is ....
  ....
- **3** The pizza wasn't bad. The burger was very bad.
  The pizza was ....
  ....

UNIT 12

SUPERLATIVE ADJECTIVES

→ **See Grammar reference, Unit 11, Comparative adjectives, p.153**

Adjective	Superlative
One syllable	
young →	the youngest
Two syllables with consonant + -y	
heavy →	heavier
Two syllables or more	
famous →	more famous
Irregular	
good →	the best
bad →	the worst
far →	the farther / further

- We use superlative adjectives to compare one thing with two or more other things.

  *The Hopper computer is one of **the fastest** in the world.*

- We use **the** before the superlative adjective.

  *This is **the** smallest mobile phone you can buy.*

- When we talk about a place with the superlative adjective, we usually use **in**.

  *This is **the most expensive** laptop **in** the world / **in** my city / **in** my town, etc. (**not** ~~of the world~~)*

Spelling

→ **See Grammar reference, Unit 11, Spelling: comparative adjectives, p.153**

The spelling rules for superlative and comparative adjectives are the same.

- **One-syllable adjectives:**
  - mostly add *-est.*
    *small → small**est**, cheap → cheap**est***
  - if they end in *-e*, add *-st.*
    *nice → nice**st**, late → late**st***
  - if they end in consonant + vowel + consonant (except *w, x* or *y*), double the consonant and add *-est.*
    *big → bi**gg**est, fat → fa**tt**est*

- **Two-syllable adjectives** ending in consonant + *-y* change the *-y* to *-i* and add *-est.*
  *busy → bus**i**est, happy → happ**i**est*
- **Two or more syllables** add **most**.
  *expensive → **most** expensive*

Practice

1 Write the comparative and superlative forms of the adjectives.

0 slow *slower, the slowest*

1 near ....
2 large ....
3 thin ....
4 friendly ....
5 happy ....

6 beautiful ....
7 good ....
8 bad ....
9 far ....

2 Complete the sentences with the superlative form of the adjective in brackets.

1 My sister's got .... (long) hair in my school.
2 Cristiano Ronaldo is one of .... (famous) football players in the world.
3 You can eat .... (good) burgers in my town in Ray's Burger Bar.
4 Mrs Peters is .... (friendly) teacher in my school.
5 My house has got .... (big) garden in my street.
6 Last night we saw .... (funny) film in the world. I laughed a lot!

3 Write sentences with superlative adjectives.

0 The supermarket / busy shop / my town
  The supermarket is the busiest shop in my town.
1 The cheetah / fast animal / world
  ....
2 Russia / large country / world
  ....
3 Salad / healthy food / this café
  ....
4 I / bad singer / my class
  ....
5 My brother / good player / his team
  ....

4 Circle the correct words to complete the sentences.

1 I think history is *more / the most* interesting than science.
2 Travelling by plane is *faster / the fastest* than travelling by bus.
3 Whales are *heavier / the heaviest* animals.
4 Jupiter is *bigger / the biggest* planet in the solar system.
5 A Rolls Royce is *more / the most* expensive than a Renault.
6 Mount Everest is *higher / the highest* mountain in the world.

UNIT 13

SHOULD/SHOULDN'T

Positive
I/You/He/She/It/We/They **should go** to bed earlier.
Negative
I/You/He/She/It/We/They **shouldn't (should not) play** tennis.
Questions
What **should** I/you/he/she/it/we/they **do**?
Should I/you/he/she/it/we/they stop doing sports?
Short answer
Yes, I/you/he/she/it/we/they **should**.
No, I/you/he/she/it/we/they **shouldn't**.

- We use **should** and **shouldn't** to give advice.
  *'I've got a headache.' 'You **should take** some medicine. You **shouldn't listen** to loud music.'*
- We use **should** to say something is a **good idea**.
  *'My hand hurts.' 'You **should go** to the doctor.'*
- We use **shouldn't** to say something is a **bad idea**.
  *'I feel sick.' 'You **shouldn't eat** anything.'*
- After **should** and **shouldn't**, we use the infinitive without **to**.
  *'My leg hurts.' 'You should **rest** and you shouldn't **walk**.'*
  (**not** ~~you should to rest … you shouldn't to walk~~)

Practice

1 Complete the sentences with *should* or *shouldn't*.

1 John's got a temperature. He .... go to school.
2 I hurt my foot. The doctor says I .... play football for three weeks.
3 My best friend didn't pass the exam. His teacher thinks he .... study harder.
4 If your back hurts, you .... go swimming. It's very good for you.
5 My sister lost her mobile yesterday. I think she .... go to the police station.
6 If you want to enter a race, you .... start training the day before the race.

2 Write complete sentences with *should* or *shouldn't* and the words in the box.

> ~~do sport and exercise~~
> drink a lot of cola and lemonade
> eat a lot of sweets and chocolate
> eat healthy food
> sleep well
> spend a lot of time watching TV

If you want to keep fit and healthy, …
0 you should do sport and exercise.
1 ....
2 ....
3 ....
4 ....
5 ....

3 Write complete questions with *should*. Then write the short answer.

0 I / run a race? (✔)
   Should I run a race?
   Yes, you should.
1 my brother / buy a fast car? (✘)
   ....
   ....
2 my friends / go to bed earlier? (✔)
   ....
   ....
3 we / have a party? (✔)
   ....
   ....
4 I / enter the competition? (✘)
   ....
   ....

4 Read the situations and write some advice with *should* or *shouldn't*.

0 I don't feel well. What should I do?
   You should go to bed and lie down.
1 It's my mum's birthday next week. What should I buy her?
   ....
2 I've got an exam tomorrow. Should I study all night?
   ....
3 I want to visit another country. Where should I go?
   ....
4 My brother wants to do a new sport. Which one should he do?
   ....
5 I want to make some new friends. Should I join a club?
   ....

UNIT 14

PREPOSITIONS

We can use **prepositions** to say where things are.

A river goes through *the town.*

Three bridges go across *the river.*

The post office is next to *the train station.*

The train station is beside *the post office.*

The car park is in front of *the supermarket.*

The petrol station is opposite *the library.*

The restaurant is near *the train station.*

The hospital is outside *the town.*

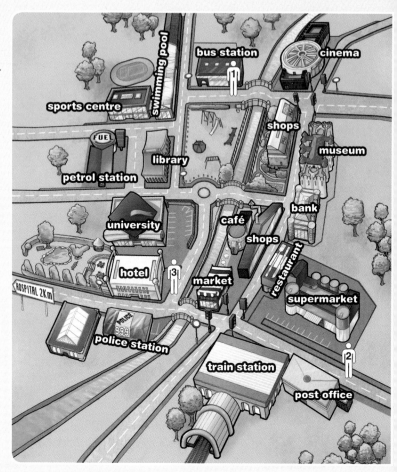

Practice

1 Look at the map of the town. Circle the correct words to complete the sentences.

1 The swimming pool is *near / across* the bus station.
2 To get to the train station, walk *across / through* the bridge.
3 The university is *opposite / next to* the library.
4 The petrol station is *beside / near* the university.
5 The cinema is *opposite / next to* the river.
6 There's a car park *in front of / through* the supermarket.

2 Look at the map again and complete the sentences with the words in the box.

| across   near   next to   opposite   outside   ~~through~~ |

0 A river goes ....through.... the town.
1 .... the town, there's a hospital.
2 Drive .... the bridge and there's a cinema on your left.
3 There's a roundabout .... the middle bridge.
4 The park is .... the police station.
5 The café is .... the bank.

3 Read the questions and write true sentences about your town.

0 Where's your school? ....*It's near my house, opposite the park.*.......
1 Is the hospital outside your town? ....
2 What's your favourite shop? Where is it? ....
3 Does a river go through your town? ....
4 How often do you walk across a bridge? ....
5 Is there a museum in your town? Where is it? ....

UNIT 15
PAST CONTINUOUS

Positive	I/He/She/It **was eating** dinner.
	You/We/They **were playing** football.
Negative	I/He/She/It **wasn't (was not) sleeping**.
	You/We/They **weren't (were not) helping**.
Questions	What **was** I/he/she/it **doing** at 8 am?
	What **were** you/we/they **watching** on TV?
	Was I/he/she/it **playing** computer games?
	Were you/we/they **listening** to music?
Short answers	Yes, I/he/she/it **was**.
	No, he/she/it **wasn't**.
	Yes, you/we/they **were**.
	No, you/we/they **weren't**.

We use the **past continuous** to talk about activities happening at a moment in the past.
*I **was watching** TV, my parents **were working** and my brother **was playing** football yesterday afternoon.*

→ See Grammar reference, Unit 2, Spelling: *-ing* form, p.144

Practice

1 Circle the correct words to complete the sentences.

1 At 6 pm, I *was doing / were doing* my homework.
2 My mum *was cooking / were cooking* when I got home.
3 Yesterday afternoon, we *wasn't playing / weren't playing* tennis.
4 When I saw you, you *wasn't wearing / weren't wearing* your new cap.
5 My friends *wasn't having / weren't having* lunch at 1 pm.
6 We *was climbing / were climbing* a tree on Saturday morning.

2 Complete the text with the past continuous form of the verbs in the box.

> bark   listen   ~~make~~   not sleep
> not watch   rain   read   sit   use

When I woke up this morning, my dad **(0)** ...*was making*... breakfast. The dog was hungry so he **(1)** ....
My sister was in her bedroom. She **(2)** ....; she **(3)** .... a magazine. My mum and my brother **(4)** .... the computer. My grandma **(5)** .... in her favourite armchair but she **(6)** .... TV. The neighbours **(7)** .... to loud music. I looked outside the window and it **(8)** .... so I decided to stay at home.

3 Write complete questions in the past continuous. Then write the short answer.

At 10 am yesterday, ...
0 it / snow? (✗)
...*was it snowing?*...
...*No it wasn't.*...

1 your friends / ride their bikes? (✔)
....
....

2 you / shop with your friends? (✔)
....
....

3 your mum / work? (✗)
....
....

4 I / have a shower? (✗)
....
....

5 you and your friends / study at school? (✔)
....
....

4 Put the words in order to make questions. Then write true answers.

0 yesterday at 11 am / you / were / sleeping / ?
Were you sleeping yesterday at 11 am?
No, I wasn't. I was studying at school.

1 were / doing / you / at 8 am this morning / what / ?
....
....

2 blue socks / you / were / wearing / yesterday / ?
....
....

3 after school yesterday / watching / a film / were / you and your friends / ?
....
....

4 raining / was / it / yesterday evening / ?
....
....

5 on Saturday morning / what / your friends / doing / were / ?
....
....

UNIT 16

PAST SIMPLE AND PAST CONTINUOUS

→ See Grammar reference, Units 5–7, Past simple, p.147–149

→ See Grammar reference, Unit 15, Past continuous, p.157

- We use the **past continuous** to describe activities happening at a particular moment in the past. Sometimes these activities happen at the same time. We're not interested when the activities started or finished.

  *John **was looking** at the gorillas and his sister **was buying** an ice cream.*

- We use the **past simple** when one complete action follows another.

  *I **woke** up and I **went** downstairs.*

- We often use the **past simple** and **past continuous** together to say that one action interrupts another.

  *A gorilla **was eating** some fruit when the boy **fell**.*

when and while

When we use the **past simple** and **past continuous** together, we often use:

- **when** before the past simple.

  *The boy was looking at the gorillas **when** he fell.*

- **while** before the past continuous.

  ***While** the boy **was looking** at the gorillas, he fell.*

Practice

1 Circle the correct words to complete the sentences.

1 When the teacher *came / was coming* into the classroom, we *played / were playing* cards.

2 She *didn't sit / wasn't sitting* on the sofa when she *heard / was hearing* a strange noise.

3 While I *walked / was walking* to school, it *started / was starting* to rain.

4 John *arrived / was arriving* while my sister *made / was making* breakfast.

5 My brother *climb / was climbing* a tree when he *fell / was falling*.

6 I *didn't meet / wasn't meeting* my teacher while we *shopped / were shopping*.

2 Complete the sentences with when or while.

1 I was tidying my bedroom .... you phoned me.

2 We found some money .... we were playing outside.

3 I wasn't doing anything .... you phoned.

4 .... you sent me the message, I was doing an exam.

5 My mum was swimming in the sea .... someone stole her purse.

6 .... my friends were snowboarding, they saw a famous musician.

3 Complete the sentences with one verb in the past simple and one verb in the past continuous.

1 My teacher .... (travel) by boat when she .... (feel) sick.

2 When the music .... (start), I .... (not talk) to my friends.

3 While I .... (carry) the plates, I .... (fall).

4 We .... (run) in the park when we .... (see) a large dog.

5 While I .... (do) my homework, my phone .... (ring).

6 We .... (not visit) the British Museum while we .... (stay) in London.

4 Complete the sentences so they are true for you. Use the past simple or the past continuous.

0 When I woke up yesterday, *it was raining.* ....

1 While I was going to school, ...

2 When I got to school, my friends ....

3 The teacher came into the classroom while ....

4 When I arrived home, ...

5 While I was doing my homework, ...

UNIT 17

FUTURE WITH *GOING TO*

- We form the '*going to*' future with **be** + **going to** + **infinitive without to**.

Positive
I'm (am) **going to phone** our friends.
You/We/They**'re** (are) **going to invite** all our friends.
He/She/It**'s** (is) **going to watch** the concert.

Negative
I'm (am) **not going to do** any homework.
You/We/They **aren't** (are not) **going to buy** pizza.
He/She/It **isn't** (is not) **going to record** the concert.

Questions
Who **am** I **going to see**?
What **are** you/we/they **going to do** later?
Where **is** he/she/it **going to go**?
Am I **going to have** fun?
Are you/we/they **going to phone** me later?
Is he/she/it **going to tell** Mum and Dad?

Short answers
Yes, I **am**.   No, I'm **not**.
Yes, you/we/they **are**.   No, you/we/they **aren't**.
Yes, he/she/it **is**.   No, he/she/it **isn't**.

- We use the '*going to*' **future** to talk about our future plans or intentions.
  I'm going to watch the concert this evening.
  We aren't going to study next weekend.

- We usually decide about our future plans before we use the '*going to*' future.
  Where are you going to go next summer?
  Mum bought the tickets last week. We're going to visit Paris and Berlin.

- We often use future time expressions like **this evening, tomorrow morning, next summer, when I'm 18**, etc. with the '*going to*' future.
  I'm going to travel when I'm 18.
  My dad isn't going to drive us to school tomorrow morning.

Practice

1 **Write complete sentences with the '*going to*' future.**

0 I / buy / new trainers.
   ..*I'm going to buy new trainers*.. .

1 We / not ride / our bikes to school tomorrow.
   ....

2 My friends / watch / the talent show on TV.
   ....

3 My mum / not play / tennis later.
   ....

4 My dad / make / pizza.
   ....

5 My cousins / not visit / us next weekend.
   ....

2 **Complete this paragraph with the '*going to*' future form of the verbs in the box.**

buy	~~fly~~	not go	not serve
stay	travel	watch	work

Next summer, I **(0)** ...*'m going to fly*.. to Canada with my family. We **(1)** .... with our cousins. I **(2)** .... a football shirt for my cousin Jack because he likes sport. We **(3)** .... a football match with him. I love travelling. When I'm 18, I **(4)** .... to university. I **(5)** .... around the world. I **(6)** .... as a shop assistant in different countries but I **(7)** .... food in a restaurant. That's hard work!

3 **Complete the questions with the '*going to*' future form of the verbs in brackets.**

1 What .... you and your friends .... (do) after school today?

2 What .... you .... (wear) tomorrow?

3 .... your mum .... (work) next Saturday?

4 Who .... you and your family .... (see) at the weekend?

5 .... your friends .... (travel) to another country next summer?

6 .... you .... (study) in another town when you're 18?

4 **Write true answers to the questions in Exercise 3.**

1 ...*We're going to ride our bikes.*...

2 ....

3 ....

4 ....

5 ....

6 ....

UNIT 18

MAKING SUGGESTIONS

- A **suggestion** is a plan or an idea that you want someone to think about.

  Why don't we go to the concert?

  Shall we meet outside the cinema?

  Why not ask your mum to drive us?

  Let's go to a restaurant later.

- After **Why don't we …, Shall we …, Why not …** and **Let's …**, we use an infinitive without *to*.

  *Shall we **make** a cake?* (**not** ~~Shall we to make~~)

  *Why don't we **buy** some lemonade?* (**not** ~~Why don't we to buy~~)

- **Why don't we …, Shall we …** and **Why not …** are questions so we use a question mark (**?**).

  *Why not go by bus**?***

  *Shall we meet at 8 pm**?***

- **Let's …** is a sentence so we use a full stop (**.**).

  *Let's go to the football match**.***

- When someone makes a suggestion, we often use expressions like **Cool!, Sounds good!, You're right!, Good one!** and **Excellent idea!** to answer.

  'Let's go swimming!' 'Cool!'

Practice

1 Circle the correct words to complete the suggestions.

  1 Let's *use / to use* that computer over there.

  2 *Shall we / We shall* include some cartoons in the magazine?

  3 *Let's / Why not* ask our teacher to help.

  4 *Why not / Shall* we play hockey?

  5 *Let's / Why not* write down our ideas first?

  6 *Why don't we / Why we don't* put a notice on the website?

2 Write suggestions with *Shall …, Why not …* and *Let's …* and the words in the box.

  | have | ~~listen~~ | read | ride | take | watch |

  0 ..*Why not listen*.. to music?

  1 .... the film on TV.

  2 .... we .... pizza for dinner?

  3 .... our bikes to school tomorrow?

  4 .... the book before we see the film.

  5 .... we .... some photos in the museum?

3 Read the sentences, then write a suggestion.

  1 It's my birthday tomorrow.

  ....

  2 We haven't got any homework to do today.

  ....

  3 The school holidays start next week.

  ....

  4 I'm bored and it's raining.

  ....

  5 I'm hungry and there isn't anything to eat.

  ....

  6 We have to do something for the school magazine.

  ....

UNIT 19

HAVE TO / DON'T HAVE TO

Positive	I/You/We/They **have to get up** early.
	He/She/It **has to share** a bedroom.
Negative	I/You/We/They **don't have to go** climbing.
	He/She/It **doesn't have to wear** a uniform.
Questions	What **do** I/you/we/they **have to do** now?
	What time **does** he/she/it **have to get** up?
	Do I/you/we/they **have to bring** snacks?
	Does he/she/it **have to wear** nice clothes?
Short answers	Yes, I/you/we/they **do**.
	No, I/you/we/they **don't**.
	Yes, he/she/it **does**.
	No, he/she/it **doesn't**.

- We use **have to** to talk about necessity or obligation.
  I can't go out. I **have to help** *my mum.*
  We **have to be** *at school at 8 am for the school trip.*

- We use **don't have to** to say something is not necessary.
  It's Saturday. You **don't have to get up** *early. (But you can if you want.)*
  My cousins **don't have to wear** *a uniform at their school.*

Practice

1 Circle the correct words to complete the sentences.

1 You *have to train / has to train* hard to enter a race.
2 My school is opposite my house. I *don't have to go / doesn't have to go* by bus.
3 We *have to leave / has to leave* our phones at home.
4 You *have to mix / has to mix* eggs and milk together to make pancakes.
5 My dad *don't have to wear / doesn't have to wear* nice clothes at work.
6 You *don't have to make / doesn't have to make* breakfast. I can do it.

2 Complete the sentences with the correct form of *have to* and the verbs in the box.

| do   not bring   not buy   not help   stay   ~~tidy~~ |

0 Every morning, I ....*have to tidy*.... my bedroom.
1 You .... any milk. There's a lot in the fridge.
2 My friends are lucky. They .... at home.
3 We .... a vocabulary test every week at school.
4 My brother is ill. He .... in bed today.
5 You .... anything to my party. I've got a lot of food and drink.

3 Write complete questions with *have to*. Then write the short answer.

0 you / study hard at your school? (✔)
  Do you have to study hard at your school?
  Yes, I do.

1 your mum / wear a uniform at work? (✗)
  ....
  ....

2 you / turn off your mobile at school? (✔)
  ....
  ....

3 your dad / travel for his work? (✗)
  ....
  ....

4 we / do Exercise 5? (✗)
  ....
  ....

5 your friends / make their beds? (✔)
  ....
  ....

4 Complete the questions with the correct form of *have to* and the verb in brackets. Then write true answers for you.

0 ...*Do*... you *have to go* (go) to bed early on Saturday night?
  ....*No, I don't*................ .
1 What time .... you ....
  (get up) on a school day?
  ....
2 .... you .... (speak)
  English in your English class?
  ....
3 How much homework .... you and
  your classmates .... (do)
  every day?
  ....
4 What .... you .... (do) if
  you miss a class?
  ....
5 .... you .... (buy) a ticket
  before you get on a bus in your town?
  ....

UNIT 20

ADVERBS OF MANNER

- We use **adverbs of manner** to say **how** we do something.

  *You have to speak **quietly** here.*

  *My sister can play the piano **beautifully**.*

- We make many adverbs of manner by adding *-ly* to the adjective (see Spelling below).

  *My little brother is **noisy**. He does everything **noisily**.*

  *I'm very **careful**. I always do my homework **carefully**.*

- There are some irregular adverbs.

  good → well, fast → fast, hard → hard

Spelling: adverbs of manner

Most adverbs add *-ly* to the adjective.	*quick → quick**ly***
For adjectives ending in *-l*, we double the *l* in the adverb form.	*beautiful → beautifu**ll**y*
For adjectives ending in consonant + *-y*, we remove the *-y* and add *-ily*.	*easy → eas**ily***

Practice

1 **Write the adverb form of the adjectives.**

0 slow	....*slowly*....	**4** quiet	....	**8** bad	....
1 careful	....	**5** wonderful	....	**9** angry	....
2 good	....	**6** heavy	....	**10** fast	....
3 happy	....	**7** hard	....	**11** noisy	....

2 **Complete the sentences with the adverb form of the adjectives in the box.**

> bad   careful   good   hard   ~~loud~~   quick

0 I can't hear you. The band is playing very ....*loudly*...... .

1 If you want to pass the exam, you have to study ....

2 My brother won the race because he ran very ....

3 Please don't ask me to draw a picture. I draw ....

4 Listen ....! I'm going to repeat these instructions.

5 Let's have dinner at your house. Your dad cooks really ....

3 **Complete the questions with the adverb form of the adjectives in brackets. Then write true answers for you.**

0 Which famous musicians sing ..*beautifully*.. (beautiful)?

  ..*I think Rihanna sings beautifully.*..................

1 How many languages can you speak .... (good)?

  ....

2 How often do you do your homework .... (slow) and .... (careful)?

  ....

3 Do you eat .... (quick)?

  ....

4 How far is your school from your house? Can you walk there .... (easy)?

  ....

5 Do you play in a sports team? Does it play .... (bad) or .... (good)?

  ....

List of irregular verbs

Infinitive	Past simple
be	was, were
become	became
begin	began
break	broke
bring	brought
build	built
burn	burned/burnt
buy	bought
catch	caught
choose	chose
come	came
cost	cost
cut	cut
do	did
draw	drew
dream	dreamed/dreamt
drink	drank
drive	drove
eat	ate
fall	fell
feel	felt
find	found
fly	flew
forget	forgot
get	got
give	gave
go	went
grow	grew
have	had
hear	heard
hit	hit
hold	held
hurt	hurt
keep	kept
know	knew
learn	learned/learnt
leave	left

Infinitive	Past simple
lend	lent
lie	lay
lose	lost
make	made
mean	meant
meet	met
pay	paid
put	put
read	read
ride	rode
ring	rang
run	ran
say	said
see	saw
sell	sold
send	sent
show	showed
shut	shut
sing	sang
sit	sat
sleep	slept
speak	spoke
spell	spelled/spelt
spend	spent
stand	stood
steal	stole
swim	swam
take	took
teach	taught
tell	told
think	thought
throw	threw
understand	understood
wake	woke
wear	wore
win	won
write	wrote

Acknowledgements

The authors would like to thank Annette Capel and Alyson Maskell for their support and guidance throughout the project.

The authors and publishers are grateful to the following for reviewing the material during the writing process:

Brazil: Litany Ribeiro; Spain: Laura Clyde and Patricia Norris; Turkey: Yucel Akgun, Ali Bilgin and Marion Oner.

Development of this publication has made use of the Cambridge English Corpus, a multi-billion word collection of spoken and written English. It includes the Cambridge Learner Corpus, a unique collection of candidate exam answers. Cambridge University Press has built up the Cambridge English Corpus to provide evidence about language use that helps to produce better language teaching materials.

This product is informed by English Profile, a Council of Europe-endorsed research programme that is providing detailed information about the language that learners of English know and use at each level of the Common European Framework of Reference (CEFR). For more information, please visit www.englishprofile.org

The authors and publishers acknowledge the following sources of copyright material and are grateful for the permissions granted. While every effort has been made, it has not always been possible to identify the sources of all the material used, or to trace all copyright holders. If any omissions are brought to our notice, we will be happy to include the appropriate acknowledgements on reprinting.

Daniel Seddiqui for the adapted text on p.42 from 'Living the Map, 50 jobs in 50 States'. Copyright © www.livingthemap.com. Reproduced with permission; Stephen Warren-Smith and Adam Dale Kilpatrick for the adapted text on p.48. Copyright © www.crazyguyonabike.com. Reproduced with permission; Snorgtees.com for the adapted text on p.64. Copyright © www.snorgtees.com. Reproduced with permission.

For the sound recordings on p.24: Tracks 1.20 and 1.21: *One Eyed Cat* by Pete Levin and the Paddlewheelers. Copyright © Pump Audio/Getty Images; *Bach – Orchestral Suite no.3 'Air on a G String'* by Charles Roland Berry. Copyright © Pump Audio/Getty Images; *Oh My Soul 90* by Elias Music Library. Copyright © Elias Music Library/Getty Images; *Meet Me In Vegas* by Rinat Arinos. Copyright © SoundCloud/Getty Images; *Strain Beatz – Dead Flow – Feat G-One* by Joel Greenwood. Copyright © SoundCloud/Getty Images; *Execution* by John Pregler. Copyright © Position Music/Getty Images, p.110, Track 2.48: *I Got The Blues* by Tribe Of Noise. Copyright © SoundExpress/Getty Images; *Ripped Apart* by Elias Music Library. Copyright © Elias Music Library/Getty Images; *Island Love* by Elias Music Library. Copyright © Elias Music Library/Getty Images; *Celtic Wind* by Danny Infantino. Copyright © Pump Audio/Getty Images.

Photo acknowledgements

p.11 (TR): cristovao/Shutterstock; p.13 (TL): Tatiana Popova/Shutterstock, (T swim): BlueOrange Studio/Shutterstock, (T cake): CandyBox Images/Shutterstock, (TR): Jacek Chabraszewski/Shutterstock, (BL): Odua Images/Shutterstock, (C): li jianbing/Shutterstock, (BR): Nejc Vesel/Shutterstock, (R): picturepartners/Shutterstock, 14 (1): PhotoStock10/Shutterstock, (2): David Shih/Shutterstock, (3): Andrey_Popov/Shutterstock, (4): Ady Kerry/Alamy, (5): muzsy/Shutterstock, (6): Anastasios71/Shutterstock, (7): Maridav/Shutterstock, (8): Africa Studio/Shutterstock, (9): Talashow/Shutterstock, (10): Nickolya/Shutterstock, (BR): Inspirestock/Corbis, (BL): Michael Austen/Alamy; p.16 (TL): Robert Harding Picture Library Ltd/Alamy, (TC): muzsy/Shutterstock, (TR): Jack Hollingsworth/Blend Images/Corbis, (CL): Scott Takushi/AP/Press Association Images, (BL): Dario Lopez-Mills/AP/Press Association Images; p.19 (TL): Bon Appetit/Alamy, (TR): Blaine Harrington III/Corbis, (B): Geoffrey Robinson/Alamy; p.20 (TL): Tracy Whiteside/Shutterstock, (BL): Design Pics Inc.- RM Content/Alamy; p.22 (CR): John Lander Photography/Alamy, (TR): Pixel 8/Alamy, (C): fotohunter/Shutterstock, (CL): IndiaPicture/Alamy, (BL): Arisha Singh/Shutterstock, (main): Mikhail Kolesnikov/Shutterstock; p.23 (T): Patrick Swan/*/Design Pics/Alamy, (b): Hemis/Alamy, (c): dbimages/Alamy; p.26 (TC) & (1): Ted Foxx/Alamy, (2): Caro/Alamy , (3): Roger Bamber/Alamy (4): Andrey Armyagov/Shutterstock; p.31: arek_malang/Shutterstock; p.32 (TL): digitallife/Alamy, (TR): Francisco Martinez/Alamy, (CL): PhotoEdit/Alamy, (CR): PSL Images/Alamy, (B): Michael Kemp/Alamy; p.33 (T): used with permission of Microsoft, (B): Nestle UK; p.35 (TL), p. 52 (TC), (TR) & p. 61 (C): Radius Images/Alamy, p. 35 (TR): Monkey Business Images/Shutterstock; p.36 (a): Gareth Copley/PA Archive/Press Association Images, (b): The Gallery Collection/Corbis, (c): Sony Music Archive/Getty Images, (d): Bettmann/Corbis, (e): Martin Keene/PA Archive/Press Association Images, (f): 2002 Topham Picturepoint/topfoto, (g): Pictorial Press Ltd/Alamy, (h): Sharok Hatami/Rex, (i): Dennis Hallinan/Alamy, (j): Roger Viollet/Getty Images; p.38 (a): The Art Gallery Collection/Alamy, (b): Bikeworldtravel/Shutterstock, (c): Dan Brreckwoldt/Shutterstock, (d): The Gallery Collection/Corbis; p.42 & p.43: Daniel Seddiqui/livingthemap.com; p.44 (T): AfriPics.com/Alamy, (C): Jeff Greenberg/Alamy, (B): Cultura Creative (RF)/Alamy; p.46 (a) & p. 49 (BL): Jacek Chabraszewski/Shutterstock, p.46 (b): De Visu/Shutterstock, (c): Kathrin Ziegler/Getty Images, (d): Pushish Donhongsa/Shutterstock, (e): hxbbzxy/Shutterstock, (f): oliveromg/Shutterstock, (g): Joy Brown/Shutterstock, (h): Graffizone/istockphoto; p.47: Songquan Deng/Shutterstock; p.48 (TR): Tim Graham/Getty Images, (TL): Swen Pfortner/dpa/Corbis, (CL) & (B): Stephen Warren-Smith and Adam Dale

Kilpatrick/crazyguyonabike.com; p.50 (TR): Front cover of MATILDA by Roald Dahl. (First published by Jonathan Cape 1988, Puffin Books 1989, 2001, 2007). Text copyright Roald Dahl Niminee Ltd, 1988. Illustrations copyright Quentin Blake, 1988, (CR): Front cover of JAMES AND THE GIANT PEACH by Roald Dahl (Puffin, 2007). Text copyright Roald Dahl p.66 (B): nito/Shutterstock, (TC): Richard , 1961. Illustrations copyright Quentin Blake, 1995, (C) & p.108 (TR): Front cover to be used in its entirety of CHARLIE AND THE CHOCOLATE FACTORY by Roald Dahl (Puffin Books, 2001, 2007, 2013). Text copyright Roald Dahl, 1973. Illustrations copyright Quentin Blake, 2001, p.50 (CL): image courtesy of The Roald Dahl Museum and Story Centre/roalddahlmuseum.org, (BR) & p. 66 (TR) & p.88 (4), p.88 (B) & p. 92 (TR): Getty Images; p. 50 (BL): Time & Life Pictures/Getty Images; p.51: Andreas von Einsiedel/Alamy; p.52 (TL): Blend Images/Alamy, (BL): Time & Life Pictures/Getty Images; p.51: Andreas von Einsiedel/Alamy; p.52 (BL): michael seman/Alamy, (BC): Dariush M/Shutterstock, (BR): Elizabeth Whiting & Associates/Alamy; p.53: Stephen Rees/Shutterstock; p.54 (a): INTERFOTO/Alamy, (b): R.W. Wood/National Geographic Society/Corbis, (c): SSPL via Getty Images, (d): Museum of Flight/Corbis; p.56: MO_SES Premium/shutterstock; p.60 (1): SWNS.com, (2): Robert George Young/Getty Images, (3): Patrick Ryan/Getty Images, (4): Jason DeCrow/AP/Press Association Images, (5): Mark Boulton/Alamy; p.61 (L): Catchlight Visual Services/Alamy, (R): MBI/Alamy; p.62 (TL): Aardvark/Alamy, (TR): maximimages.com/Alamy; p.64: www.snorgtees.com; Cummins/Corbis; p.67: B Christopher/Alamy; p.69: Isaac Koval/Getty Images; p.70 (TR): David Noton Photography/Alamy, (CR): dbimages/Alamy, (L): David Noton Photography/Alamy, (BR): National Geographic Image Collection/Alamy; p.71 (T): Stan Kujawa/Alamy, (CL): National Geographic Image Collection/Alamy, (CR): Keren Su/China Span/Alamy, (BL): VPC travel Photo, (BR): Foodio/Shutterstock; p.72 (TL): Seth Wenig/AP/Press Association Images, (TR): Jmiks/Shutterstock, (BR): Lawrence berkeley National Lab-Roy Kaltschmidt, photographer, (BL): Pictorial Press Ltd/Alamy; p.75: incamerastock/Alamy; p.81: Larisa Lofitskaya/shutterstock; p.84 (T): Holmes Garden Photos/Alamy; p.86 (BR): Rob van Esch/Shutterstock, (BL): Zdenek Krchak/Shutterstock, (BC): Paul Thompson Photography/Alamy; p.88 (1): The Gallery Collection/Corbis, (2): Georgios Kollidas/Alamy, (3): Akademie/Alamy; p.89: Sipa Press/Rex; p. 90 (a): Paul Bock/Alamy, (b): (apply pictures)/Alamy, (c): Lsokol/Shutterstock, (d): Sundraw Photography/Shutterstock, (e): Alex Segre/Alamy, (f): behindlens/Shutterstock, (g): Hollygraphic/Shutterstock, (h): Gelpi JM/Shutterstock; p.92 (R): Michele Falzone/Alamy, (C): yogesh more/Alamy, (L): Jonathan Dorey/alamy; p.93 (TR): elementals/shutterstock; p.94 (TL): D. Virtser/Shutterstock, (TC): dpa picture aliance/Alamy, (TR): Doug Ellis/Shutterstock; p.96: www.waterrescuedogs.com/SICS Italian School of Canine Lifeguards/AP/Press Association Images; p.99 (T): D'ARCO EDITORI/Getty Images, (B): Philip Carr/fotolibra; p.102 (TR): Robin Beckham/BEEPstock/Alamy; p. 104 (T): FremantleMedia Group Ltd., (C): PictureGroup/Rex, (fans): Rui Vieira/PA Archive/Press Association Images, (judges): KenMcKay/Thames/FreemantleMedia Group Ltd/Rex, (B): Mark Allan/AP/Press Association Images; p.108 (TL): Paramount/The Kobal Collection, (B): Warner Bros. /The Kobal Collection; p.109: anshar/shutterstock; p.110 (BR): Marques/Shutterstock, (L): Mark Bassett/Alamy; p.111 (TL): Papilio/Alamy, (TC): Leo Mason/Corbis, (TR): Arco Images GmbH/Alamy, (BL): Marc Francotte/TempSport/Corbis, (BC): Chuck Pulin/Splash News/Corbis, (BR): Rohit Seth/Shutterstock; p.112 (TR): keith morris/Alamy, (CR) & (BL): Kumar Sriskandan/Alamy, (BC): Kuttig-RF-Kids/Alamy, (BR): Jonathan Goldberg/Alamy; p.113: Sergey Novikov/Shutterstock; p.114 (TR): Marmaduke St. John/Alamy, (CL): Steve Skjold/Alamy, (C): keith morris/Alamy; p.115 (L): Mark Bassett/Alamy, (TC): Roger Bamber/Alamy, (BC): Tim Graham/Alamy, (TR): Oredia/Alamy; p.116 (CL): Diana Healey/Getty Images (CR): INTERFOTO/Alamy; p. 118: Barcroft Media via Getty Images; p. 119 (L): Image Source/Alamy, (C): MBI/Alamy, (R): Image Source/Alamy; p.120 (L): Oleg (RF)/Alamy, (C): Zhiltsov Alexandr/Shutterstock, (R): Chris Fourie/Shutterstock; p.125 (T): Robert Fried/Alamy, (C girl): Blend Images/Alamy, (C boy): BSIP SA/Alamy, 125 (B): eStock Photo/Alamy; p.127 (TL): Zygotehaasnobrain/Shutterstock, (TR): YAY Media AS/Alamy, (BL): Juice Images/Alamy, (BR): Jeffrey Blackler/Alamy; p.128: David Lefranc/Kipa/Corbis.

Commissioned Photography by Gareth Boden: p.10, p.11 (L), p.13 (Jack), (Ravi) & (Molly), p.18, p.21, p.24, p.26 (TR) & (BR), p.46 (BL) & (BR), p.62 (B), p.77 (BR), p.82, p.90 (BL), p.106 (B), p.107, p.115 (BR).

Our special thanks to the following for their help during location photography: Bags ETC, Parkside Federation Academies, The Park Sportscentre, University of Cambridge Sports Centre

Front Cover photo by: R. Legosyn/Shutterstock

Illustrations

Ilias Arahovitis (Beehive Illustration) pp. 17, 30, 34, 41, 97; Nigel Dobbyn (Beehive Illustration) pp. 20, 28, 29 (B), 30, 49, 68 (R), 79 (L), 94, 95; Mark Draisey pp. 35, 57, 63, 73, 79 (BR), 80, 101, 105, 123; Mark Duffin pp. 96, 121 (B); Richard Jones (Beehive Illustration) pp. 21, 29 (T), 40, 78, 84, 85, 121 (C); Jamie Pogue (Bright Agency) pp. 27, 39, 65, 68 (L), 77, 80 (B); Martin Sanders (Beehive Illustration) pp. 42, 86, 93, 98, Pablo Velarde pp. 58, 59, 102, 103.

The publishers are grateful to the following contributors: text design and layouts: emc design Ltd; cover design: Andrew Ward; picture research: Ann Thomson; audio recordings: produced by IH Sound and recorded at DSound, London; Grammar reference section: Emma Heyderman.